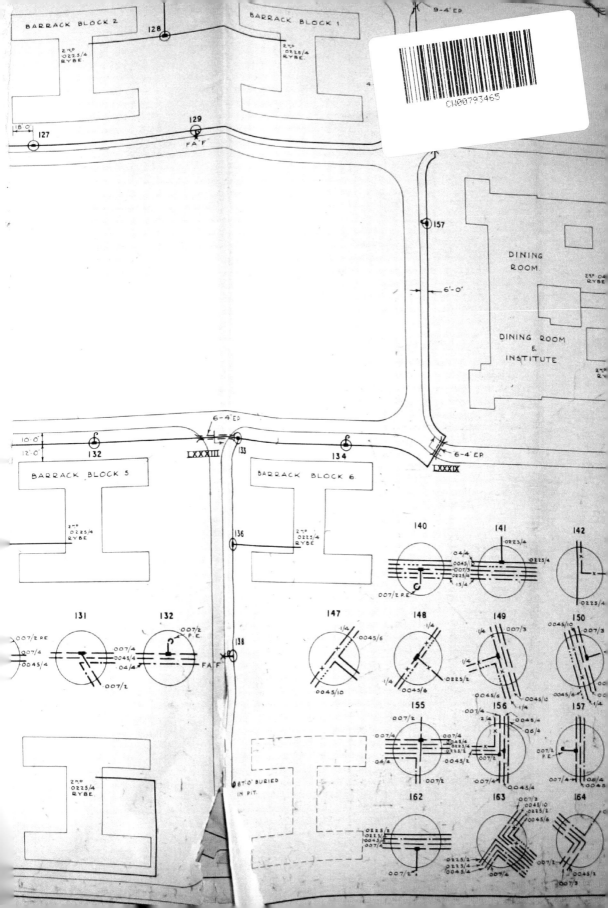

LAST POST AT
NEWT⊕N

The life of Royal Air Force Newton

Timothy O'Brien GAvA

TOBBIT

DEDICATION

To everyone who served at Royal Air Force Newton.

First (collectors) edition published 2008.
Second (revised) edition published 2009.
Published by Tobbit Publishing,
E-mail: tobrienart@hotmail.com
Website: www.timobrienart.co.uk

ISBN 987-0-9555189-1-1

Design and art direction by T J O'Brien.

Layout/design by Russell Strong.

Printed in Great Britain by the MPG Books Group, Bodmin and King's Lynn

Contents

Newton, 8th August 2008.
T O'Brien

Foreword

by Group Captain C B Adcock BA FIMGT RAF (Retd)
Station Commander, Royal Air Force Newton 1993 to 1995.

Like many flying stations, Newton had its origins in the great expansion of the RAF that took place in the years leading up to the Second World War. The airfield itself and the supporting infrastructure of control tower, hangars, and domestic buildings all conformed to a standard set of plans. These plans not only gave the station its form and function but they also gave it what we now regard as a distinctive wartime look and feel. As the war progressed, and larger and heavier aircraft came into service, geographical constraints prevented the station from being developed further. The grass airfield was, however, retained as a suitable location for flying training, a role that continued at the station until the day it closed. Consequently, through an accident of history, and probably more so than any other unit in the RAF, Newton retained the look and feel of an authentic wartime station right up to its very last day.

Although its wartime framework continued to exist, the station was nevertheless further shaped and moulded by the exigencies of post-war defence policy. The early 1960s, in particular, saw Newton enter the missile era, when the station was extensively upgraded to cater for a large expansion in technical training. Somewhat ironically, in later years, when the size of the RAF, along with its sister services, was drastically reduced in a series of defence cuts, the station survived because of its excellent training facilities and the high quality of its supporting infrastructure. Following a concomitant reduction in the requirement for technical training, a number of diverse training organisations, displaced from other stations that were closing as part of the general run down of the RAF, took up residence at Newton, thereby utilising the surplus accommodation and facilities that had become available. By the 1990s, the station had become notable not only for the evocative wartime feel of its infrastructure but also for the eclectic nature of its training task. During this era it certainly lived up to its motto 'We Teach and We Learn'.

In April 1993, however, when I took command of RAF Newton, a decision had already been taken to close the station under what was known at the time as the Ground Training Rationalisation Scheme. Consequently, much of my time and energy during my tour was taken up with preparing plans for the run-down of the station and, with the help of my staff, in maintaining the morale of the personnel, both service and civilian, at a time of great uncertainty. This endeavour was eventually brought to a close at the end of March 1995 with a Dining-In Night in the Officers Mess followed by a Sunset Ceremony and the playing of the Last Post that formally marked the end of Newton's status as a fully-fledged RAF station.

The history of Newton is therefore of general as well as particular interest, because it reflects in microcosm the sweeping organisational and social changes that affected the Royal Air Force during the second half of the 20th Century.

Through meticulous and comprehensive research, the author, Timothy O'Brien, has brought to light in this well-written and informative account the fascinating details of these developments, and highlighted them with graphic and moving first-hand accounts from many of the participants in the events. The resultant narrative presents a significant and heart-warming chapter in the history of the Royal Air Force, and I commend it to you.

C B Adcock, Salisbury.

Above: **Scottish Aviation Bulldog, XX694 (E) of East Midlands Universities Air Squadron** over **Royal Air Force Newton, circa 1983. This view clearly shows the classic 'Expansion period' layout of the airfield and grass runways. The River Trent can be seen in the top left of the photograph snaking through the valley past the village of Shelford, below the 'Bomb dumps'.** via J Martin

Left: **A wartime aerial photograph of RAF Newton, circa 1945.** EMUAS collection

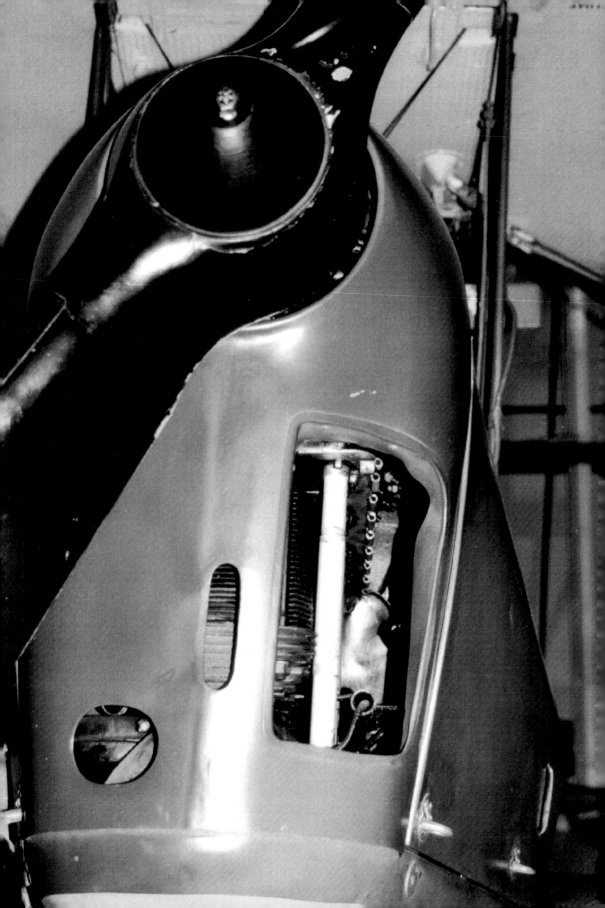

Above: **White out, mid 1990s.** Max Shortley

Left: **The Gipsy Major engine on the DH Tiger Moth.** T O'Brien

Introduction

by Group Captain Hugh F O'Neill, DFC and bar, RAF (Retd).
Served with HQ No.12 Group, Newton 1947 to 1950.

I arrived at Newton in 1947 for what turned out to be a three-year posting on the
Air Staff of Headquarters, No.12 Group in fighter Command. Like many others I
had relinquished my acting rank in the post-war shake up and I had mixed
feelings about the promise of life behind a desk. Also, I was due to fill a dead
man's shoes as my predecessor had just been killed in a mid air collision during a
Fighter Command exercise. However, my previous appointment had been in 12
Group so many of the people at Newton were friends and I quickly settled in to
the happy and welcoming atmosphere I found there.

During my posting, we were lucky to have two amiable and relaxed AOCs – Air
Vice Marshals Traill and Harcourt-Smith – and their attitude was reflected
throughout the Group. There was also a happy relationship between the Group
Headquarters and Newton itself on which we were a lodger unit.

The main thing which made life tolerable for those of us desk-bound was the
presence of a well-stocked communication flight run by the New Zealander Flt Lt
Johnny Gibson who had flown in the Battle of Britain. The flight stabled a Meteor
VIII, the only Spitfire XIV with a contra-rotating airscrew, Hornet, Oxford,
Anson, Proctor and Tiger Moth. When life in the office became too tedious, and
with encouragement from the AOC, it was customary to spring into the air either
to visit an outstation or just to beat the air with some aerobatics. This well suited
Teddy Donaldson, the Senior Air Staff Officer, who had made his name leading
the pre-war RAF Hawker Fury Aerobatic Team. He regarded the Spitfire as his
personal mount and many mornings would see him take off, turn upside down
and disappear down the sloping airfield boundary.

The length of the grass airfield presented a problem for the Meteor and Vampire,
so an extension was made into the rough and this allowed the two types to
operate safely, albeit subject to precise airmanship. Nevertheless, some people
who were used to long runways were not entirely happy with the size of Newton.
An unfortunate station commander, arriving for an AOC's conference,
approached too slowly in his Hornet and the aircraft finished up in small pieces at
touch-down. He was not a very happy chap at the meeting.

Above: **This painting titled 'The Aerial Joust' features the 1950 air race at Newton's 'At Home' day on 16th September 1950, organised by Hugh O'Neill. The winner, Flt Sgt R J Collins in his Harvard from No.22 FTS, Syerston is just ahead of Air Vice-Marshal G Harcourt-Smith in his Vampire I, with Tempest, Meteor, Seafire, Beaufighter and other types in hot pursuit.** Artist – T O'Brien GAvA

Right: **The cover of the 1950 programme featured a Vampire completing an improbably tight turn round one of the Headquarters Race pylons.** H F O'Neill collection

ROYAL AIR FORCE
NEWTON

BATTLE OF BRITAIN
"AT HOME"

Saturday
September 16th
1950

PROCEEDS TO
ROYAL AIR FORCE
BENEVOLENT FUND

Souvenir
Programme

1/-

It is fair to say that Newton had a pronounced operational atmosphere at the time as many people on the staff had had a distinguished war. These included Wing Commanders and Squadron Leaders Bill Blackwood, Joe Singleton, Wilfred Clouston, Joe Pegge, Frank Carey, John Wray and Pat Hancock. This, coupled with a lively sporting and social scene, made for a jolly, happy and interesting posting.

Timothy O'Brien has put together this incredibly detailed and comprehensive history of the station for which I have the greatest admiration. Reading it has been an exercise in nostalgia and I finish by saying how much I enjoyed my time at Newton.

H F O'Neill, York.

Above: **Flying in DH Tiger Moth, DE978, RUN-B, sporting its new silver livery and red wheel covers having shed its wartime camouflage, student Desmond Penrose and his Instructor from Nottingham University Air Squadron are seen over Belvoir Castle, Leicestershire, 1948.** Artist – T O'Brien GAvA

ALERT STATE

Prelude

Through the searchlights and indiscriminate bursts of flak, a tempest of shells and bullets ripped into the Wellington bomber of 103 Squadron. The New Zealand born pilot, Flying Officer Robert Chisholm, took evasive action swiftly to try and save his crew, while his front and rear gunners opened fire at the German night-fighter. Up there, high above Dutch territory with nowhere to hide, they just had to sit there and fight for their lives. It had been ninety minutes since they took off into the night sky from the grass runways of Royal Air Force Newton at 2300 hours on 12th June 1941. Their objective had been to bomb the marshalling yards and signalling system at Osnabruck in North West Germany and so far, apart from the hazy conditions on the bombing run, they had been blessed with good fortune. But now it was the early hours of that most notorious of dates, Friday 13th and their luck was to run out. More bullets pierced the fuselage and the two Bristol Pegasus engines as Ofw Hans Rasper of 4./NJG1 came in for the kill. At 0037 hours Wellington T2996 crashed into a field belonging to Mr Langendijk, 10km west of Enkhuizen in Noord Holland with no survivors amongst the six-man crew.

Sixty one years later in June 2002, Elvis had returned to top the charts with 'A little less conversation', communities came together across England to celebrate the Queen's Golden Jubilee, and indulge in World Cup mania. However for several rural communities, one topic of conversation that summer was of Asylum Seekers. The Home Office had announced their plans to build the first of three accommodation centres housing 750 refugees on Ministry of Defence land at Throckmorton in Worcestershire, Bicester in Oxfordshire and at RAF Newton in Nottinghamshire.

Such plans threatened to shroud these sites in controversy, ignoring their more illustrious past. Each one has many stories, but the site at Newton is particularly interesting, being a bomber base before the Polish Air Force moved in to use the grass runways. This forged such strong connections between the Free Polish Forces and Newton, that it was later incorporated into the station's crest featuring the White Polish Eagle and the motto 'Docemus et Discimus', meaning 'We teach and we learn'. This training theme was to remain with the base for the rest of its military career.

When flying ceased on November 10th 2000, RAF Newton, once affectionately nicknamed 'Sleepy Hollow' by local MP Kenneth Clarke, had the distinction of being the last operational RAF station in Nottinghamshire and the last RAF airfield with three fully operational grass runways with full-time Air Traffic and Fire cover in the United Kingdom. This leaves the gliding schools at Syerston as the last RAF presence in the county today. It is ironic that in the late sixties both stations faced the axe, but somehow Newton survived while Syerston 'closed', only to remain on a care and maintenance basis. However in the end Syerston has outlived Newton as Ministry of Defence (MoD) property and for flying activity.

Above: **The scene across the Trent Valley from Oatfield Lane today. The 'smug and silver Trent' wriggles out of sight behind the trees and church at Shelford. It is hard to imagine that this serene typical English village played a savage episode in the Civil War. The Crown land in this photograph is currently under threat of large scale gravel extraction!** T O'Brien

Right: **The public protest in Bingham's Market Place during June 2002, where local residents voiced their opposition to the Government's proposed Asylum Seeker Centre at the former RAF Newton that had closed the previous year.**
Artist – T O'Brien GAvA

Remembering what it used to be like at Newton, the station has now taken on an eerie, silent atmosphere as you walk around the main camp looking at the shabby buildings and long grass. There were 700 personnel working here in the early nineties who brought the scene on the ground to life, while the Chipmunks and Bulldogs animated the sky overhead. Now there is only the occasional film crew who use two of the hangars as a studio and apart from a handful of other businesses and farmers the base is largely derelict. The only sound today is that of the wind as I walk past some deserted tennis courts in front of the water tower.

It's hard to believe that only a few years have passed since RAF Newton was a thriving self-contained 'village' in a rural location. The community was also constantly adaptable to change over sixty years, depending on how global events shaped the bigger picture beyond this corner of Nottinghamshire. The community spirit that existed within its boundaries also spread outside to enrich the lives of the local population and will be forever imprinted on local folklore. But more than anything it is the human side of the story, the tales of heroism, joy, laughter and tragedy that bring the history alive. This story is not intended to be the definitive study, but will hopefully give an idea of what life was like on a Royal Air Force station in the 20th century.

To set the scene, the tiny village of Newton is situated in South-East Nottinghamshire, amidst fields belonging to the crown, while the airfield itself sits on a plateau overlooking the Trent Valley to the North. Looking up the valley towards Newark, you can still see gliders soaring out of the plateau at Syerston, four miles away. To the West of Newton behind 'No Joke' wood is the large commuter village of Radcliffe-on-Trent. Along the Southern boundary is the Nottingham to Skegness railway line, while the small market town of Bingham is 1 mile to the East and beyond the charming Vale of Belvoir, famous for its Stilton cheese stretches out to the South East. However for all its beauty this area is no stranger to change and conflict throughout history. A few hundred yards away near Newton Springs, the Romans created a military settlement called 'Margidunum' which survived until about 450 AD. Today the site lies near a traffic island on the A46 'Fosse Way', another legacy of the Romans invasion of Britain and despite the ominous military presence it would have had a bonus in providing a marketplace for local farmers and industry. Then in the mid 4th century Germanic tribes, Angles, Saxons, Picts and Scots from the North and Ireland all took turns at raiding the area.

With the routes along the River Trent, Fosse Way and the Great North Road all passing through the region, the area continued to be a decisive one to control in later conflicts such as the English Civil War. Newton was sited in an uncomfortable position between the Parliamentarian base at Nottingham and the Royalist sites at Newark and Belvoir. Down in the valley 100 feet below Newton and the derelict windmill is the village of Shelford, a Royalist stronghold that witnessed several tenacious battles between Cavaliers and Roundheads. The River Trent whose Celtic name of 'Trisantona' meaning 'trespasser', can then be seen snaking its way down from Newark, behind Shelford then on up the valley

Above: **Stan Wright in front of 'No.2 Hangar'
in August 2002.** T O'Brien

Right: **The crash gate on the Shelford Road
by the old windmill.** T O'Brien

Bottom: **Newton's windmill today. The
derelict wooden structure was dismantled
at the end of the war. Another windmill,
now a private residence can be seen in the
distance in the neighbouring village of East
Bridgford.** T O'Brien

to the old Saxon settlement of Nottingham, where the Civil War actually began on 22nd August 1642 with Charles 1st raising his standard at the castle to rally support. Over the next three centuries the area remained largely agricultural with only the industrial revolution and the coming of the railway having any obvious impact on the rural way of life.

As part of the treaty of Versailles after the Great War of 1914-1918, Germany was forbidden to operate a substantial air force. So as no immediate threat remained, Britain began to rundown its military strength into a much leaner force for the post-war years that followed. That is, until Adolf Hitler became Chancellor of Germany in 1933 and started his extensive rearmament programme including the creation of a new air force. Alarm bells then started to ring out across Britain and the rest of Europe. After all it was still less than twenty years since the First World War and memories were still fresh, especially those of the Zeppelin raids on British towns and cities. Like a sleeping lion provoked with a sharp stick, Britain reacted to this new threat by building up its own military strength again to act as a deterrent. By the mid 1930s, the community around Newton cautiously anticipated the future, as they knew that life was going to dramatically change as the government had plans for their part of rural England.

Circa 1936 the Air Ministry started purchasing the 595-acre site at Newton in three phases as part of the RAF's 'expansion scheme'. This was a massive programme to build permanent aerodromes across the country, in response to what was happening in Nazi Germany. While the majority of fighter bases were constructed in the south, the eastern counties of England were to house the new bomber stations, with Newton being one of them.

One family living at Newton that were going to feel directly the impact of this new airfield were the Wright family living at 'Newton Fields' Farm sited on the plateau near the old windmill. They had been there since 1934, when they had moved from East Leake so Mr Wright could take on the 28-acre smallholding. When his twin sons left school they started working for him on the farm. In 1938 Mr Wright secured a contract to provide six horse and carts on a daily basis to carry materials around the airfield construction site. His son Stan used to drive one of the carts, often moving surplus soil from the concrete perimeter track. On a wet and windy afternoon in August 2003 I arranged to meet Stan by the old guardroom and armoury. Leaving his car parked in the layby next to the patch of grass once occupied by the Hawker Hunter gate guardian, Stan gets into my car. Before we drive off for a tour of the base I ask Stan about the public's reaction in the 1930s to the news that the airfield that was going to be built on their doorstep, *"well it was quite different in those days, I suppose there wasn't much you could do about it so you just accepted it and got on with it"*. As we drive off we follow several cars full of 'Robot Wars' fans heading towards a hangar to be the audience for another series that is being filmed. As we turn left by the Station Headquarters to follow the one-way system, Stan looks at the H Blocks on the left and the technical blocks on the right and comments, *"what strikes me is the amount of buildings, they are colossal and everything is overgrown. Along this road there were no buildings back then in 1938, just the contractors huts, the site office and lots of Irish labourers. The contractors were called 'Constable Hart' and I remember that they used to store some materials and equipment near our farm along the Shelford Road. As the road had been closed to the public any labourers who needed access along here had to pass a sentry box and show their passes. Many just used to say that they were with 'Constable Hart' and walk through. I remember the frustrated sentry once saying 'that's the fourth today, the next bugger that comes here claiming to be with 'Constable Hart' I'm going to ask him who this Policeman is!' Apart from moving soil in my cart I remember helping to stack and cover piles of bricks in the store that were brought in by the London Brick Company on 20 ton rigid 8 wheel lorries."*

When work began at Newton a Roman Villa was found close to the 'Margidunum' site which also suggested a civil as well as a military presence. In its own way RAF Newton was to become a 20th Century military fortress guarding the Trent valley just as 'Margidunum' and the castles at Nottingham and Newark had done centuries earlier.

We turn left into the road by the empty space where the red telephone boxes once stood. On the left stands the Airmen's Mess and NAAFI club while to the right it overlooks the parade square cum car park. We travel down the road by the H blocks once occupied by the RAF Police Museum and Headquarters Air Cadets then stop at the far end near the Community Centre. Looking at a sealed up air raid shelter next to it Stan comments, *"I remember they built shelters for all the civilian properties too that stood within a certain radius of the station including our farmhouse".* Across the road stands the station sick quarters and decontamination centre surrounded by pallets full of canvas and metal frames belonging to a marquee company. The medical centre still has traces of wartime camouflage painted on the bricks like a faded tattoo around the sash windows. This pre-war 'expansion period' of 1934-1939 gave the government a chance to construct a range of military sites and buildings that complied with a uniform style. Standard building designs were drawn up around a clean Georgian style so that the same type could be reproduced in brick at many sites. However with the later requirements for bomb blast protection, 'late expansion period' buildings favoured concrete rather than brick construction.

Just as planning regulations have to be observed today, back in the 1930s the Preservation of Rural England advised on the location of all these military buildings in relation to the neighbouring countryside, while the designs of individual buildings were subject to review and approval by the Royal Fine Arts Commission. The buildings at all these sites can be divided into four distinct groups of which Newton is a classic example. The technical buildings, communal and barracks were all located together on the main site, while the fourth, the bomb store was located well away from these buildings for safety reasons. Newton's 'bomb dumps' are sited on the edge of the plateau that overlooks the Trent Valley.

Due to the late start in construction, the five 'C' type (Protected) hangars were built in 1938 as the utility version with more concrete and less bricks used. As we drive up the road towards the hangars and the airfield Stan remembers the first hangar roof being installed on Good Friday, "*I remember it well as I was helping to plant some trees. They may have got the doors up that day as well. The trees were Black Poplar or Manchester Poplar which is a tree that is very quick growing and always blows in the wind*". Passing a farmer tending some sheep on the airfield, we stop in front of the hangars by the control tower. Stan looks out over the airfield and recalls "*over there in the middle of the airfield was the 'Keepers Cottage' where Mr Needham used to live. He was employed by the Crown Estate and his cottage was the very first building to be demolished when construction began*". All the remaining buildings on the camp were the usual sand coloured brick types and painted with a green and black camouflage, the remains of which can still be seen today on some barrack blocks. The large grass landing strip comprised of three intersecting runways with the main runway being aligned to the prevailing winds and fitted with landing light equipment while the two shorter runways crossed the main one to make a triangle shape. Around the runways a perimeter track was constructed along with 'frying pan' aircraft dispersal points branching off into the surrounding fields and woodland. These dispersals were mainly concentrated on the southern side due to the landscape falling away sharply to the north down into the Trent Valley, however there were a few on the northern edge, with one being near the derelict windmill. This is also the site of 'Newton Fields' Farm where Stan lived. The ground crews used to push the aircraft out by hand through the 'crash gate', across the road and into the dispersal point next by the farmhouse, air raid shelter and Nissan hut. By the perimeter track there are also four defensive pill boxes located on the North, South, East and Western edges of the airfield and can all still be seen in the undergrowth today.

Such a massive construction project like the one at Newton, gave a welcome boost to the local economy through the various contractors involved. In Roman or medieval times local stonemasons and blacksmiths would have been employed, but it would now be the turn of bricklayers, electricians, plasterers, plumbers and joiners. In 1936, the approximate financial cost of building an airfield like Newton was £550,000. One of the local firms that benefited was the Barnstone Cement Company based on Works Lane in Barnstone. From here the firm's first lorry driver, Fred Bower of Bingham used to take cement in his 8-ton lorry to the construction site at Newton around 5 to 6 times a day for several weeks. Once construction was complete the base continued to provide employment for numerous civilian trades over sixty years such as administrative staff, window cleaners, tailors, barbers, bar staff, milkmen, coach firms, maintenance and catering staff. As well as Stan Wright who was now part of the scenery travelling around the base on his cart pulled by his horse 'Sandy'.

"RAF Newton, once affectionately nicknamed 'Sleepy Hollow' by local MP, Kenneth Clarke"

Photographed from a Chipmunk is this
aerial view of RAF Newton circa 1991,
looking east towards Radcliffe-on-Trent.
Note how neat and crisp everything looks,
especially the grass runways, compared to the
contemporary views elsewhere in this book.
T O'Brien

An aerial view of RAF Newton taken on 8th August 2008 from former Newton resident, Firefly G-BUUE, now based at Tollerton. Note how the cut-grass runways have disappeared. The market town of Bingham is to the right of the picture. T O'Brien

**Ken Wallis and 'Little Nellie'
in 2003.** T O'Brien

The Way to the Stars

As a maelstrom of bullets streaked out of the stars, Sgt Hamblin swiftly retaliated by cranking round his rear turret to aim the 0.303 Browning machine-guns at the assailant. After a loud burst of fire from the Wellington's guns, their attacker fled into the darkness. While Hamblin kept watch from his cold, lonely turret, his 'boss', Squadron Leader Mellor assessed the damage to 'Sierra Leone' as they crossed the English coast. This particular machine from 103 Squadron (Sqn) was a 'presentation aircraft', having been paid for by funds from the West African state. Now back in home skies, they descended towards Newton's grass runways. Having touched down, something was wrong as the edge of the runway rapidly approached. Due to the loss of brake pressure they ran out of runway, crashing to a halt near the bomb dumps. The crew's beloved 'Sierra Leone' was a write off.

However the name was given a second chance as another Wellington, PM-G was christened 'Sierra Leone II' a few days later, although it didn't bring better luck than the last. On the night of 30th March 1941, 'Sierra Leone II' again piloted by Sqn Ldr Mellor, took off at 1900 hours for a bombing raid over Brest. Their target, the two pocket battleships *Scharnhorst* and *Gneisenau*, which if damaged would stay in dock instead of making a dash onto the high seas. With the operation complete they headed back and as they prepared to land at Newton around 0025 hours the following morning, they were 'welcomed' with a hail of fire from a German Junkers Ju88 'night intruder' that had invited itself into the circuit. Another Wellington came under fire as it landed. The intruder missed it, hitting the flare path instead before turning its attention to Mellor's aircraft. Unfortunately Sgt Stewart, the front gunner and Sgt Hamblin, the rear gunner had just vacated their turrets moments before as per the standard practice prior to landing. Badly damaged, with the pilot, co-pilot and wireless operator injured, 'Sierra Leone II' approached the airfield and force-landed in a ploughed field ½ mile from the airfield near East Bridgford.

Two years earlier, during the summer of 1939, the grass landing strip at Newton was ready for emergency use and according to Stan Wright the first aircraft to land was an Armstrong Whitworth Whitley, whether it was intentional or by accident, no one knows. When war ignited in September 1939, it was first used as a 'scatter field' to disperse twelve Handley Page Hampdens evenly split from 49 and 83 Squadrons at RAF Scampton, Lincolnshire. Nicknamed the 'Flying Suitcase' because of its appearance, the Hampden was a delight to fly but didn't live up to its role of a bomber. During this period after the fall of Poland until April 1940, better known as the 'Phoney War', aircraft of Bomber Command started a limited bombing offensive against military targets only and dropped propaganda leaflets, which several locals remember seeing bundled into Hampdens at Newton.

Not only had the landscape altered, the local way of life had changed too with hundreds of servicemen being deposited onto a site that was until recently just farmland. And some of them certainly announced their arrival in a dramatic way. On 18th May 1940 during a training flight from Newton, Sergeant Pritchard of 83 Sqn overshot the runway in Hampden L4059 and crashed on the edge of the airfield in woods near Oatfield Lane, leaving a distinct gap in the trees which could still be seen from the village of Shelford until very recently. Amazingly the crew survived unhurt, which unfortunately cannot be said for the two crew members on board Avro Anson Mk1, N5096 of 49 Sqn. Having taken off on a training flight on 4th October 1939, they were seen to climb to 100 feet before diving into the ground near Radcliffe-on-Trent with fatal consequences.

Still unfinished, the base officially opened on 3rd July 1940, having been allocated to No.1 Group. During that day the first operational aircraft, Fairey Battles of 103 and 150 Squadrons flew in. Earlier, in August 1939, these squadrons along with other units of this Group had been mobilised to France as an Advanced Air Striking Force (AASF) equipped with obsolete Battle aircraft. Amongst the many reconnaissance and bombing missions, both units attacked the bridges along the River Meuse during May in an attempt to stall the German advance. But, after putting up a gallant fight against overwhelming odds and heavy losses, the tattered remnants of the squadrons were recalled home to England in June 1940, with 103 Sqn going to Honington, Suffolk and 150 Sqn to Stradishall, Suffolk. Then as the units of No.1 Group started to recover from this retreat from France, they relocated their Group Headquarters (HQ) to RAF Hucknall, Nottinghamshire and both squadrons soon followed by making their way to Newton.

According to Sid Finn's book *Black Swan*, a history of 103 Squadron, the choice of RAF Newton as their new base was a welcome one, as the airfield was a modern RAF station with excellent facilities; brick built accommodation along with well equipped canteens. All in all it was a comfortable base and only ten miles from Nottingham. Both squadrons quickly settled in by having a mess party, with food being supplied by local farmers and washed down with some bottles of wine that had returned from France with them and of course, plenty of attractive local girls! But as the base was still relatively new and not enough quarters for everyone, some airmen were billeted in private residences in Bingham and Radcliffe and in some cases along with their wives. One house in Radcliffe had just installed a new telephone and occasionally it would ring with a message from Newton for the 'lodger', who then ran round to other houses scrambling the rest of the crew.

With Wing Commander T C Dickens in charge of 103 Sqn and Wing Commander A G Hesketh DFC commanding 150 Sqn, both units spent their time settling into Newton by scrounging fittings and furniture to help get themselves functioning properly, as the base was still being completed by the contractors. Time was also taken to exchange war-weary aircraft with new ones and repair others to get the units back to operational strength. With this new equipment the squadrons were now starting to get back on their feet, rebuild morale and would soon be ready to combat Hitler's invasion of the British Isles.

On 10th July 1940 Air Marshal Sir Arthur Barratt and Air Vice Marshal P H L Playfair flew into Newton to inspect the two squadrons on parade in a hangar and spoke to individual aircrew before flying out after lunch. Later that day the station was put on standby as Invasion Alert No.1 came into force. With both units participating, a flight of six aircraft were put on constant readiness from dusk till dawn, with the duty air and ground crew sleeping in the hangar annex. However this only lasted a week before the units commenced night operations. The first of these operational sorties from Newton took place during the night of 16th July when Wg Cdr Dickens of 103 Squadron led three of his aircraft out over the North Sea to attack oil storage tanks at Rotterdam. But due to low cloud over the target area the Battles dropped their bombs on a chemical works and an aerodrome instead. 150 Sqn undertook its first 'op' on the night of 21st / 22nd July by joining 103 and other units to form part of an 81 aircraft mission to attack 7 targets over Germany, Holland and France. This sortie was the largest night bombing raid since the fall of France and the first major operation by Fairey Battles of Bomber Command.

During the 25th and 26th July 1940, yet more aircraft arrived as Newton played host to Fairey Battles and Hawker Hurricanes of 98 Sqn that were staging through the region to take up coastal patrol duties in Kaldadarnes, Iceland. Like many other units they too had only recently returned from France and were now being redeployed. However the squadron was not a total stranger to the skies of Nottinghamshire as they had been stationed at nearby Hucknall from August 1936 to March 1940 before they departed for Scampton.

From July to the September both 103 and 150 Squadrons mainly carried out raids concentrated against the anchorages, ports and harbours of Belgium, France and Holland. These targets were a top priority as the location of a vast number of barges and small craft commandeered from Germany and the occupied countries and now brought together for the planned invasion of Britain, codenamed 'Operation Sea Lion'. The Luftwaffe also attempted to gain control of the air during what was to become known as the Battle of Britain. As a result of a call up for volunteers several pilots from Newton were transferred to fighter duties to help win this battle in the air. In return Naval aircrew were posted to Newton for around three months as Midshipmen pilots and Petty Officer Observers.

Having now become operational with a boosted morale, it wasn't long before tragedy struck. In the churchyard of St Peters in the neighbouring village of East Bridgford are two headstones of some unlucky souls who did not even start their operation. They are Flight Lieutenant Walter M Blom DFC of 150 Sqn, a 23 year-old pilot from Peterborough and Sgt William Franklin BEM of Radlett, the son of a Naval Commander. Walter Blom had only recently been decorated for bravery in France with the AASF and was one of the few to have survived this episode. On Saturday 27th July 1940, a bomb fell from their Fairey Battle L5528 whilst being 'bombed up' and began to burn. Despite attempts by the crew who were inside the aircraft at the time to extinguish the flames, assisted by a number of ground crew and headquarters staff, the bomb exploded killing the three-man aircrew and four groundcrew. Five others were left with severe injuries with one dying the following day. For William Franklin's parents it was a double tragedy as their second son had also died whilst serving his country.

When they weren't facing danger on operations or letting off steam at the Unicorn Hotel by the River Trent at Gunthorpe, both squadrons undertook an intensive training programme at Newton. They practised low level bombing runs against targets on the side of the airfield well clear of the hangars. The aircraft were also fitted with spray bars so the aircraft could simulate mustard gas attacks against enemy targets. As a harmless substitute, the aircraft sprayed a water / aniseed mixture, which was picked up by disc markers on the airfield perimeter near the old windmill to register the spray density during a simulated attack. But thankfully in the end these attacks never happened for real. Meanwhile the Battle of Britain was building up to its climax and the targets for 103 and 150 Squadrons were becoming more concentrated on the invasion barges in Calais and other channel ports. Despite the target areas being easy to find, the small invasion craft proved difficult to destroy. However the relentless bombing attacks continued until October.

On 2nd October 1940, both squadrons stood down from operational duties so they could re-equip with the twin-engined Vickers Wellington bomber. Orders were given that two Battles were to be withdrawn for every Wellington that arrived. This new aircraft was affectionately known as the 'Wimpy' after the character J Wellington Wimpy in the Popeye comic strip. Designed by Barnes Wallis, the Wellington had an innovative geodetic structure. 103 Squadron's first examples arrived on the 2nd, with the remainder arriving by 24th October. Meanwhile 150 Squadron's first example was also delivered the same day, followed by the remaining aircraft on 9th October to make a total of nine aircraft on the unit. Both squadrons then began a concentrated working up period on the type before operations could recommence.

Wednesday 13th November 1940 was to prove to be an unlucky day during this training period for the two Squadrons, with their first aircraft losses since converting from Battles. Struggling to stay airborne, Wellington L7813 of 103 Sqn came into land at 1940 hours before crashing and sinking into the grass runway. Twenty-five minutes later Wellington N2998 of 150 Sqn landed across the flarepath and collided with the wreckage of the first one and burst into flames, totally destroying them both. Fortunately everyone escaped unhurt.

By the end of November, 150 Sqn was the first to return to operational duties, followed by 103 Sqn on 29th December. Compared with the low morale six months earlier both squadrons were now in good spirits as they had new aircraft and were fully operational. As the threat of invasion had receded, aircraft from Newton now turned their attention against targets in Germany and the *Scharnhorst* and *Gneisenau* in Brest Harbour as the 'Battle of the Atlantic' was now starting to gain momentum. Enemy shipping and ports continued to be the main targets until the night bombing offensive started to take the bombers deeper into Nazi Germany, attacking cities such as Dusseldorf, Hamburg, Duisberg and Hannover. If Berlin was to be the target, the Wellingtons were usually flown to RAF Stradishall or Newmarket racecourse to be topped up with fuel and a full bomb load ready for the long haul, as the foundations and length of Newton's grass runways proved unsuitable for heavily laden aircraft. However there were instances when Wellingtons carried reduced bomb loads from Newton to make sure they reached Berlin or were topped up with extra fuel when they were lined up on the edge of the runway.

With a dispersed Wellington parked at the end of Stan Wright's garden, his father's horses soon became used to aircraft noise, often standing under the wings while the engines were running on full throttle without being bothered. The noise of the engines could even be heard over the other side of the Trent valley. During the harsh winter of 1940/41, to keep the grass runways operational local farmers removed snow from the airfield at a cost of £1 a day for horse, cart and man.

Local folklore is full of tales: such as the one about the spy found in the derelict windmill; but villagers still enjoy the following: one afternoon in November 1940, the station was on full alert as a German aircraft approached at tree top level. Two bombs were released as it crossed the base. One fell behind the Airmen's Mess and embedded itself in the road. The second; a large incendiary landed on the parade ground. Both had failed to detonate! Unwisely the intruder returned: the eight Bofors anti-aircraft (AA) gun crews had now calculated the range, plus ground-crews manning aircraft gun turrets gave the German a good hiding. The UXBs: thought to have delayed action fuses, were covered in sandbags by the bomb disposal team. There was an immediate evacuation of the Mess, NAAFI, tailor's shop and surrounding buildings. All airmen were then fed from a field kitchen hastily erected some considerable distance away. 103 Sqn air-gunner, Sgt Norman 'Jock' Cameron was returning on the bus from an evening of heavy drinking in Nottingham. He happened to sit next to the intoxicated station tailor; who told him about the impending doom upon his shop if the bombs exploded. Jock decided to help his new 'pal' by 'borrowing' a two-wheeled cart and two planks. Not hearing any ticking they successfully rolled it up the planks onto the cart at the third attempt. They shook hands before trundling it clumsily around the camp. Jock wanted to deposit it on the COs doorstep, but was dissuaded by the tailor. About to leave the bomb on the sports field next to the Officers' Mess instead, the Orderly Officer appeared and in reply to his *"who goes there?"*, received *"it's only us old cock; where do you want this bomb?"*; or so the story goes! However, this urban myth was authenticated by a witness in a letter to Sid Finn, the author of *Black Swan* in October 1976 who forwarded it to Jock Cameron.

During this period of the airfield's history it was not uncommon for enemy aircraft to venture into the area and attack the airfield or even pursue aircraft. For the defence of the airfield against such attacks a number of forces were in residence with the following units recorded as being based at Newton on 13th July 1941. These were, 722 Defence Squadron RAF, C Company of the 10th Battalion, Sherwood Foresters and 112th Battery of the 28th Regiment, Royal Artillery.

A pair of Wellington bombers over St Mary's church in the neighbouring village of Radcliffe-on-Trent as they race back to Newton. Artist – T O'Brien GAvA

During another incident, members of the Trent River Patrol opened fire with their Lewis guns from a converted cabin cruiser on an enemy aircraft seen following an aeroplane into Newton. The river patrol was created in June 1940 and based in a former café at Gunthorpe this was to be the one and only time during the war when they fired their guns in anger. After this they went back to their usual target practice of firing the Lewis Gun at the red clay cliff face at Radcliffe, where bullets are still being dug out today.

A boat was to come to the rescue again for one crew of 103 Sqn. They had taken off from Newton at 1847 hours, 10th February 1941 in Wellington T2610 to successfully bomb Hannover; but had been hit by flak. On their return home; with Aldeburgh only 35 miles away one of their engines cut out and they soon lost height. The pilot Sgt Bill Crich DFM decided that their only option was to ditch. Ten feet above the North Sea, the 'Wimpy' stalled and pancaked into the ice-cold water. The crew waded through the sinking bomber to the nearest escape hatch. Sgt G Farley despite suffering a fractured collarbone hauled out air-gunner Sgt 'Jock' Cameron, who had a broken wrist. Along with Sgt L F Waern DFM, Sgt R Layfield and Sgt Geoff Chadd they turned over the capsized, partially inflated dinghy and scrambled inside. As all emergency rations had been lost when the dinghy capsized, the crew just had three bottles of water, some chewing gum and their wits for survival. Several aircraft were spotted including a Wellington conducting a square search, but they failed to attract attention. For two days the dinghy bobbed along with Bill Crich singing to boost morale amongst the frost-bitten, tired and sea-sick crew. Then, "Look out, minefield!" cried Jock Cameron; but the danger thankfully turned out to be a school of porpoise. At 2200 hours on the second day three ships steamed into sight. After several cries for help, the third ship lowered a small boat into the sea and came to the rescue. It was the Danish vessel, the SS *Tovelil*. The skipper had initially been wary about picking them up, as he thought that it was a well-known German trap, but the vessel's British machine gunner had recognised the voices of his fellow countrymen. After being given dry, warm clothes and a hot meal the aircrew were put ashore at Minster on the Isle of Sheppey.

In those early days of the war, Britain's survival depended on the maritime trading routes, especially those in the North Atlantic. But between September 1939 and May 1943 the country faced defeat almost on a daily basis during the Battle of the Atlantic as the German submarines (U-Boats), warships, merchant raiders and aircraft kept trying to sever these supply routes. On the night of 7th May 1941 aircraft of 150 Sqn bombed the massive dry docks and submarine berths in the French port of St Nazaire. Another target was the port of Lorient on France's Atlantic coast, with the aircraft taking off from Newton at 1805 hours on 21st March 1941. After completing their operation the aircraft turned for home. All returned safely apart from Wellington R3288 JN-B piloted by Flying Officer C H Elliot. Seconds after it broke through cloud cover at 2308 hours it crashed into Moel Farlwyd on the unforgiving Snowdonia. When the rescue party arrived at the crash site the next morning, they found no survivors until they spotted the rear turret lying on its own, broken off from the fuselage on impact. Rear gunner

Sgt P Martlew was miraculously still inside, suffering from a broken leg. Times like these were often anxious ones for those waiting back home at Newton and in the airmen's 'billets' in Bingham and Radcliffe. But as soon as their landlady saw a pair of flying boots in her hallway, she could sigh with relief that her lodger and his crew were home safe and well.

The following morning as Stan was driving his horse and cart he noticed the damage inflicted on the dispersed aircraft as he drove past. Due to heavy rains during February, Newton's grass runways weren't fit for operations so the Wellingtons temporarily operated out of Lindholme. In return it wasn't unusual for other aircraft to use Newton when they weren't able to operate from their own airfield. Polish manned Wellingtons from 300 Sqn at Swinderby and 304 (Silesian) Sqn based at Syerston were amongst those occasionally dispersed to Newton. As I park the car on the old aircraft apron now used as a temporary car park for the 'Robot Wars' audience, Stan Wright relates a story about them as we observe the BBMF Dakota in the distance flying into the gloom over the Trent valley on a training flight from Barkston Heath. As we get out of the car and stand on the tarmac, Stan says *"The Polish Wellingtons were parked here one afternoon while I was working nearby".* He saw that a party was in progress. The WVS and NAAFI tea wagons had arrived to provide refreshments, as the Polish crews were singing and dancing to the music of an accordion player. *"Then I saw some of the airmen disappear with some empty lemonade bottles, only to return with them full of suspicious looking liquid. All the bottles were put in a crate before being loaded into the aircraft presumably with the intention of being offloaded over Germany!"*

During June 1941 one of the new personnel posted to 103 Squadron was Pilot Officer Ken Wallis, who since the war has become well known for his autogyros and in particular 'Little Nellie' that he flew in the 1967 James Bond film 'You Only Live Twice'. Ken recalls his brief posting to Newton, *"I had been flying Lysanders with 268 and 241 Army co-operation squadrons but was one of those asked to 'volunteer' to go on Bomber operations. Consequently I converted on to Wellingtons straight from Lysanders at 20 OTU at Lossiemouth. During the conversion course I soon became the Captain of my own crew and was given the choice of three bomber squadrons. I chose 103 Sqn because it was near to Nottingham and the girls there had a special reputation! On arrival at Newton, as was the way on operational stations I had to undertake a number of operations as a second pilot before becoming a Captain with my own crew despite having my own crew at the OTU".* These flights mainly consisted of cross-country training flying, air tests, formation practice and photo bombing trips as second pilot to Pilot Officer Petrie and Pilot Officer Muggeridge. Ken remembers taking off from Newton's runways *"I certainly recall these take offs from Newton with a heavily laden Wellington on those warm summer evenings. Take-offs were almost invariably towards Nottingham with the need to clear the railway cutting at the edge of the grass field. It was not good on the nerves to look at the bending of the undercarriage legs as the poor old Wellington struggled to take off. Then having cleared the railway we would struggle to gain height as we flew over the city".*

Newton's Wellington bombers faced danger on many more occasions during their short turbulent stay, but the breeze of transition was soon sweeping across the station. The airfield at Newton could not continue to be a bomber base despite plans being drawn up to extend it including new concrete runways, extra bomb stores and a sixth hangar. But for some unknown reason the Air Ministry decided against further development, resulting in the loss of new runways being constructed. During May 1941, rumours began to circulate the base that the squadrons would eventually be moving to Lincolnshire. Which was confirmed when No.1 Group relocated to its new HQ at Bawtry Hall near Doncaster on 20th July 1941. This change was to affect the social life of local villagers who sorely missed the unit's 'Squadronaire' style band at local gala dances, held every Friday or Saturday night in the CO-OP hall at Radcliffe. By now these events had become a popular local custom until one Saturday night dance was cancelled. The move was confirmed, the squadrons were moving out of Newton and split up with 150 Sqn finally departing for Snaith in Yorkshire on 10th July, followed on the 11th by 103 Sqn who were going to Elsham Wolds, Lincolnshire.

From the beginning of July there had been a lot of movement between Newton and these new stations and a considerable amount of planning had been undertaken to move all the personnel, aircraft, spares and equipment. Ken Wallis remembers the move *"We certainly had some good times in Nottingham, but we were so soon to move to the new airfield at Elsham Wolds"*. On 11th July Ken flew out of Newton for the final time in Wellington R1446 to Elsham. *"When I arrived at the new airfield it was the first time that I had flown a Wellington from a concrete runway!*

The nearest big town to Elsham Wolds was Scunthorpe, which was not like Nottingham!" It was also time for Stan Wright to move away from their farmhouse at Newton, as his family moved to a farm at Elston, near RAF Syerston. Their farmhouse remained unoccupied on the dispersal point until being demolished just after the war.

Left: **One of the many wartime Tannoy speakers still extant on the station.**
T O'Brien

"Rumours began to circulate the base that the squadrons would eventually be moving out to Lincolnshire"

'Touch Me Not'

103 Squadron was formed on 1st September 1917 and with the squadron motto 'Touch me not', it was employed on bombing and reconnaissance raids on the Western Front. It was disbanded in 1919 before being re-formed in August 1936 with Hawker Hinds.

Above: **Fairey Battles of 103 Squadron over Gunthorpe Bridge.** Artist – T O'Brien GAvA

Right: **Sgt J E Blair in the rear turret of Wellington R1041 at Newton.** The Blair family via Mike King

Opposite page, clockwise from top left:

Joe King beside the rear turret of Wellington R1041 at Newton, May 1941. The Blair family via Mike King

The squadron mascot, 'Rastus the Owl'. via David Fell

The squadron's Black Swan motif.

The crew astride Wellington R1588 in August 1941. The Blair family via Mike King

Vickers Wellington R1588 at Elsham Wolds in August 1941, a month after the move from Newton. A veteran of 23 raids. The Blair family via Mike King

Timothy O'Brien

'Always Ahead' ✠

Brin Mason, Wireless Operator / Air Gunner, 150 Squadron.

No.150 Squadron was formed in Salonika, Macedonia on 1st April 1918 as a fighter squadron and subsequently operated in Macaedonia and Turkey. Disbanded in 1919, it was re-formed as a bomber squadron in 1938 with Fairey Battles.

Top left: **A wartime aerial view of Newton looking south.**

Centre left: **Another view taken at the same time, but looking east.**

Bottom left: **150 Squadron members in front of a Wellington in 1940. The Squadron mascot, a Bulldog called 'Pickwick' can be seen at the front.** All three Author's collection

Above: **A Wellington on finals to land following a daylight training flight. The village of Shelford can be seen in the valley.** Artist – T O'Brien GAvA

The 'Bomb Dumps'

Newton's wartime storage of explosive materials was sited away from other buildings at the far end of the airfield overlooking the Trent valley. It gained a new lease of life in the mid-1980s as a training area for the RAF Police and Regiment.

This page: **An aerial view taken in August 2008.**

Clockwise from top left:

The Windsock, Incendiary Bomb and Pyrotechnics Stores look North over the Trent valley, 1998. M & D Sibley

Large metal doors for blast protection as seen in 2002. T O'Brien

Concrete blast protection, 1998. M & D Sibley

Mock painted doors in the RAF Police / Regiment weapon storage training area. T O'Brien

Interior of storage building. T O'Brien

1980s Portakabin within the weapon storage training area. T O'Brien

One of the larger storage buildings on the site. T O'Brien

The Range

Top: **Air cadets take aim one Wednesday night during May 1983.** 1936 Sqn collection

Above left: **Wartime aircraft Test Butt. Aircraft would test their guns by firing into the recess, which would have been filled with a bank of sand.** T O'Brien

Above right: **One of two buildings in Dawson's Plantation, possibly wartime magazine stores, due to their close proximity to the dispersals.** T O'Brien

Left: **CWO Steve Elton of 1936 Sqn ATC gives some instruction to a cadet on the range, during May 1983.** 1936 Sqn collection

Bottom: **Cpl Watts of 1936 Sqn ATC also takes aim with a 0.22 rifle at the targets circa 1990.** T O'Brien

Defences

Top: Pillbox No.5 on the North-West side of the airfield by the bomb dumps with a post-war addition of an Airfield Identification Beacon (AIB) or 'Pundit' which would flash red a 3-character identifier in Morse Code. M & D Sibley

Upper left: **Pillbox No.2.** M & D Sibley

Upper right: **Pillbox No.3 on private land by the Shelford Road.** M & D Sibley

Lower left: **Pillbox No.1 near Lawson's Barn Farm.** M & D Sibley

Lower right: **Pillbox No.4, an unusual L-shaped box!** M & D Sibley

Below: **A modern pillbox installed at the end of Newton Gardens; by the A46 crash gate during the late 1980s in response to the IRA terrorism threat. The house beyond the wooden bus shelter was burned down by arsonists in 2005.** T O'Brien

Take Cover!

Main picture: **A wartime air-raid shelter sited next to MT and Stores with its entrance sealed as they are prone to flooding. One of at least ten still surviving around the camp, it is understood to be a type of 'Stanton' shelter, semi-sunken with a grass covering, one entrance and one emergency escape hatch. Other buildings such as the Officers Mess and Barrack blocks had shelters built in to the cellars. The brick structure was a post-war addition to house dustbins.** Photograph by T O'Brien

The Concrete Runways that Never Came!

Opposite page, top: **Detail section of plans circa 1940/1 for the proposed concrete runways that were never built: highlighting the new perimeter track, runway thresholds, additional bomb stores and loading platforms which would have extended across Oatfield Lane and closed the road to through traffic.** Milan Petrovic collection

Station Sick Quarters

Above: **Newton's Medical Centre in 2000.** J Proudlock

Below: **A panoramic view of the Sick Quarters with air-raid shelter in front and decontamination annexe to rear.** Adam Davey

Opposite page, clockwise from top left:

The station ambulance attends an incident during the 1987 Battle of Britain 'At Home' day. T O'Brien

The Pharmacy. T O'Brien

The boiler room. T O'Brien

Building 37, the Ambulance garage and mortuary, 2008. T O'Brien

Buildings

Right: **The post-war Boiler house.**
T O'Brien

Below: **The wartime Central Heating Station it replaced. Later used by Works services and the Fire section for drying hose pipes.** T O'Brien

Bottom: **A panorama looking east through the technical site towards the airfield.** T O'Brien

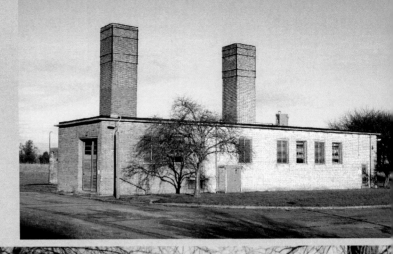

Left: **The Link Trainer building which housed a 'Link' trainer (simulator) during wartime.** J Proudlock

Below: **Station workshops designed to house an engine repair shop to the left and an airframe repair shop to the right. In the centre would be a welding shop, machine shop and blacksmiths.** J Proudlock

The Armoury

Building 27, one of the largest buildings on the technical site is a concrete structure that can be found on many former bomber stations. This bomber armoury had a photographic section on the first floor. Post-war it became the Station Headquarters while HQ No.12 Group were in residence and occupied the usual Station HQ building. Following HQ No.12 Group's departure, its use is un-clear, but could have been used for storage before it became the Regional Printing Centre and Station Photographic section until 1995. East Midlands Wing HQ and 1936 Sqn ATC then moved in during 1997 before departing in early 2001. Today it has been refurbished and painted a pale grey for commercial leasing.

Below: **A side view looking south.** T O'Brien

Bottom: **A view of the main entrance in 1994.** George Ward

Top right: **The rear entrance in 2002.** T O'Brien

Bottom right: **A fine shot of the wartime armoury, February 2008.** T O'Brien

Bomber Command's 'Early Days'

A painting by Timothy O'Brien GAvA of a Vickers Wellington of 150 Squadron (Centre), an Armstrong Whitworth Whitley (Bottom left) which was reputedly the first aircraft to land at Newton and a Handley Page Hampden (Top right) of 49 Squadron that was temporarily dispersed to Newton during 1939/40.

Warrant Officer Jozef Warchal's RAF uniform, and snapshots of him with a Miles Master at the satellite station; Tollerton. Note the Polish Eagle on the button.

'Little Poland'

Demonstrating its flexibility the station was then transferred from Bomber to Flying Training Command. With No.16 (Polish) Service Flying Training School (SFTS), moving in on 13th July 1941 from nearby Hucknall under the command of Group Captain J L Kepinski, who was one of many Poles to settle locally. The school had formed a month earlier from the Advanced Training Squadron element of No.1 (Polish) FTS and also incorporated a Polish flying instructor school within the school. As part of No.21 Group, the role of the school that was equipped with 38 Fairey Battles including a number of twin cockpit variants and 32 Airspeed Oxfords, was the advanced aspect of pilot training for the surviving Polish airmen that had escaped to England after the fall of Poland in 1939. Not only did they provide valuable information about German tactics, but reinforced the RAF during its darkest hours. Their renown for courage and fanatical determination to fight at all costs were especially noted in the Battle of Britain and early bombing campaigns. After training in England, Polish aircrews formed their own squadrons within the RAF system. However the Polish Air Force remained a separate force with its own administration under the exiled leader General Sikorski. Despite this move to Newton, the initial pilot training with the Tiger Moths of No.25 (Polish) EFTS remained at Hucknall before the advanced course at Newton. Where those intended for Bomber Command mainly flew twin engined Airspeed Oxfords and those destined for fighter Command flew single engine Miles Masters. Then from 14th August 1944, the school started using North American Harvard 11Bs mainly from the satellite stations at Tollerton and Orston. Between August 1942 and April 1943 additional support aircraft including a lone DH.42 Moth, four Avro Ansons and two Miles Magisters were also added to the SFTS inventory.

One such pilot who had escaped to England was Ted Shuvalski, who in September 1939 had been a mechanical engineering student in the south eastern Polish town of Lwów. Following the Russians entry into Poland he was sent via Kazakhstan to work on a Russian collective farm near the Chinese border. Then after a general amnesty for the Poles in 1941 following the German invasion of Russia, he travelled south to join the Polish Army at Ktasziowock. From here they crossed the Caspian Sea to Iran in barges, then onto Palestine via Iraq to strengthen units from North Africa before returning via Syria to Iraq where his unit patrolled the Turkish border. It was from here that he was selected to join the Polish Air Force after reading a circular that invited potential recruits to join. After selection he boarded the SS *Ile de France* in Suez on what was to turn into an eventful two-month sea voyage. This newly built French ship had been destined to race for the Blue Riband, but had been requisitioned in New York during September 1939. Joining the 1700 Polish Air Force volunteers on board were 6500 troops picked up in Durban, South Africa. Following another stop in Freetown, West Africa they were shadowed by four submarines, two German and two Italian. As the liner was unescorted, the Captain decided to see if she was capable to compete for the Blue Riband after all and pushed the speed from 20 knots to nearly 40 knots in an attempt to evade the slower submarines. They also altered course, resulting in

Reunited! Former Warrant Officers: Jozef Warchal and Tadeusz Kumela meet at Jozef's allotment, 1990.
Paul Kumela collection

Ted Shuvalski at Newark Air Museum in May 2003. T O'Brien

their next port of call being Rio de Janeiro in Brazil. Ted recalls, "*Most of us thought that it was because we were going so fast that we ended up here instead of England*". But due to the countries connection with Nazi spies, no one was allowed off the ship much to the troops frustration as they observed the golden beaches and women. Short of supplies they set off back to Freetown before heading to Newfoundland, then Scotland by which time everyone on board was nearly half starved. It was now 1943 and once they were safely in England they were constantly fed to build them all up to strength again. His journey would eventually take him to Newton, where he would train for the next two years to fight for his countries freedom.

Their presence was soon noticed in the local community as some Shelford residents remember hearing them jabber away in Polish and that they all seemed to have gold teeth! Aleksander Gertner, the schools first Flying Instructor said "*It was a very nice atmosphere at Newton, with good relations between the British and Polish*". Mr Gertner who had escaped the Nazis by travelling through the Atlas Mountains to Casablanca and Gibraltar before jumping on board a ship bound for England, also added "*When I arrived at Newton it was a great relief, a relief that I was going to be able to continue the fight. Everyone was very kind to us.*"

Despite the departure of the bomber squadrons, Newton was still subject to air raids. On the night of 8th / 9th August 1941 the Germans tried to bomb the airbase with incendiaries falling into the fields along the Fosse Way. Members of the Fire Service at Bingham then tried to extinguish the fires with individual metal dustbin lids! But only four bombs were actually recorded as having hit the base causing only slight damage to a Warrant Officer's married quarter.

As so many airfields were concentrated in this part of the country during wartime, it was not uncommon for other aircraft to visit Newton and practice flying 'circuits and bumps' or use it as an emergency landing strip. During the evening of 2nd October 1942, Avro Lancaster W4238 of 106 Squadron had taken off from the neighbouring airfield of Syerston at 1850 hours for a raid on Krefeld. But the crew had decided to return home early, perhaps due to a technical fault. Then at 2125 hours the mighty Lancaster approached Newton, whether by intention or by mistaking it for Syerston that was in fact four miles away. The bomber then landed on the grass runways but overshot the runway and crashed into a defence post bursting into flames. Fortunately there were no serious injuries reported amongst the seven-man crew.

During the war, Nottingham and the Trent valley were notorious for fogs and smogs especially during the autumn and winter. Which no doubt wasn't helped by the airfields location next to the River Trent. This vulnerability caused a problem during a training flight for Ted Shuvalski, as he recollects; "*I remember once during a solo flight in early 1945 when I was coming back over Leicester after having flown a triangular route to just north of London, that Newton called me on the radio and was giving me directions and I wondered why? Then I saw a black wall in front of me, it was smog and I couldn't see the airfield from 1000 feet.*" As his Airspeed Oxford was low on fuel, he was ordered to climb to 5000 feet and bail out, "*As I would have had to leave*

Main picture: **Jan Krupa in 2003.** T O'Brien

Above: **Jan and fellow mechanics by an Oxford; 1946.**
via Tim Cross

Right: **Jan in his pre-war Polish uniform.** via Tim Cross

the left hand seat and run to the rear door, by which time the unstable aircraft could have crashed, I decided against this. Instead I came down to 500 feet, and by complete coincidence I came out right above the middle of the airfield, with about ten minutes fuel left I went around and landed. As I taxied near to the hangars the engines cut out as I ran out of fuel".

The author Alan Sillitoe famous for 'Saturday Night and Sunday Morning', made his first flight here at Newton in 1943 with the Air Training Corps (ATC). In his 1987 *Nottinghamshire* book he talks about a Polish pilot taking him and some other cadets up for a twenty-minute flight over Nottingham in a DH Dominie. He also talks about eating his first 'foreign' meal in the airmen's mess and gives this as the reason for him still liking East European food.

On 1st June 1943 the numbers of aircraft recorded as being based at Newton with No.1 and 2 Training Squadrons were 26 operational (Training) and 12 reserve Airspeed Oxfords, 52 operational (Training) and 24 reserve Miles Master IIIs, 3 operational (Training) Avro Ansons plus 1 in reserve, 2 Miles Magisters and 1 Tiger Moth. There were also 6 operational (Training) Oxfords plus 2 reserves with the Beam Approach Training Flight. The station manning levels on the same date recorded 2135 personnel based on the camp and were as follows: RAF Personnel consisted of 2 Group Captains, 3 Wing Commanders, 14 Squadron Leaders, 42 Flight Lieutenants, 48 Flying Officers and 3 other officers, 11 Warrant Officers, 28 Flight Sergeants, 86 Sergeants, 166 Corporals, 647 Aircraftsman and 8 Civilians; WAAF personnel comprised of 1 Flight Lieutenant, 1 Section Officer, 1 Warrant Officer, 3 Sergeants, 11 Corporals and 76 ACWs; Polish personnel included 1 Group Captain, 2 Wing Commanders, 8 Squadron Leaders, 30 Flight Lieutenants, 40 Flying Officers, 1 other, 6 Warrant Officers, 19 Flight Sergeants, 63 Sergeants, 119 Corporals, 545 Aircraftsman and 150 Trainees.

The school was split into a number of flights, each specialising in a particular task. A student would start at 'A flight' and would visit each flight around the airfield and end up at 'K flight', which was based near the hangars. Jan Krupa was Chief Mechanic with 'A flight' and remembers one incident at a dispersal point in the book *'White Eagles'* by Phil Barton. Following a training flight a pilot left his Oxford complaining that the undercarriage warning light was still on. Later a young mechanic entered the aircraft and without thinking what he was doing, pulled the lever upwards. The aircraft collapsed causing extensive damage to the airframe. Horrified at what the consequences would be, Jan and his team decided not to report the accident. Instead they hid the Oxford amongst some trees and secretly repaired it using spares. As a result his flight earned the surreptitious title of the 'Spare plane flight' and before long, pilots were putting in unofficial requests for this spare aircraft!

Alongside the Polish air and ground crews who had their own Polish Commander some British personnel were also based at Newton being responsible to the British Station Commander. The British serviced and flew their own Airspeed Oxford, Avro Anson and Miles Magister for training purposes. From the summer of 1944 to early 1945, Lewin S Grant a Fitter 2E (Engines) was posted to this section of

Alexsander Gertner in 2003.
T O'Brien

Polish Senior NCOs during a meal in the Sergeant's Mess. WO Jozef Warchal is far left.
Jozef Warchal collection

Newton after recovering from a broken leg he had sustained in Gibraltar before being airlifted home. One story he recalls from his time at Newton is when he was working on an Avro Anson. *"A Polish chap in full flying kit walked up to the aircraft, climbed in and then asked me to get in and start the engines for him"* he recalls. They then took off bound for Hucknall, during which it transpired that the pilot was a trained aircrew member, but not actually a qualified pilot!

Lewin Grant also flew on further occasions with the Polish aircrews to other airfields at Wigsley in north Nottinghamshire and Sutton Bridge (Holbeach) in Lincolnshire. While reminiscing he also recalls hearing one story about an order that was sent for one 'Airscrew' to the massive storage depot at Stafford. A complete 'Aircrew' turned up instead, so from then on an order was issued to only refer to them as 'Propellers' to avoid any further mistakes.

As the number of aircraft on charge now approached 150, the construction of 16 'Blister' type hangars was made around the perimeter to accommodate most of them. A satellite field, five miles away at Orston and a relief landing ground at Tollerton were also used to relieve the pressure on the crowded airspace over Newton. Orston was opened with primitive facilities on farmland in 1941 exclusively for Newton's aircraft with a grass strip of 1200 yards. But after heavy rainfall the strip soon became unserviceable and was closed soon after the war. Tollerton however was an existing civilian airfield that opened in 1930 and was mainly employed by Newton when the Harvard was introduced to the school in 1944 and the aircrews and personnel were bussed in everyday from Newton.

The hectic training programme at Newton prepared many for the fight ahead, but also saw 47 Polish airmen killed in flying accidents. One example was during a formation flight of three Harvards from the school's detachment at Tollerton. One flew too close to the central aircraft and clipped the cockpit with its wing killing the pilot before the aircraft spun out of control. Not only had the aircrew paid a high price, the airfield had too, with the grass runways being worn out and deemed unserviceable. In order to maintain the flying programme whilst the runways were repaired, Headquarters No.21 Group, Flying Training Command ordered Sutton Bridge to be taken on as a satellite station. The runways also suffered in more recent times, with the top end of the airfield being prone to water logging. During the war when the same soggy problem occurred and prevented an effective flying programme, the school used the runways at Sutton Bridge again and nearby Langar, Syerston and Wymeswold. At the end of March 1944, Newton was serviceable again and No.16 (Polish) SFTS continued flying. In August 1944 the school slightly altered its title by dropping the word 'Service' to become No.16 (Polish) Flying Training School (FTS).

Newton's other occupant unit at this time was, No.1524 Beam Approach Training Flight (BATF). The BATF used eight Airspeed Oxfords (6 operational and 2 reserves) to provide training for future night-fighter and bomber pilots. This gave pilots experience at using the standard beam approach (SBA) radio beam system based upon the Lorenz Beam Devices.

Newton; November 1944.
WO Tadeusz Kumela sitting on the tail of an Oxford during a break from his refresher course.
Paul Kumela collection

TIMOTHY O'BRIEN

The Airspeed Oxford piloted by Ted Shuvalski emerges from the heavy fog directly over Newton in a miraculous piece of airmanship. Artist – T O'Brien GAvA

A wireless school was also set up in the old barn off Oatfield Lane to teach the Poles in how to communicate by radio in English. Henry Clough, the RAF Instructor remembers how he used to catch the train from West Hallam via Nottingham to Radcliffe, then cycle up to the barn every morning and open up for business, then cycle home again at night without venturing on to the main camp; apart from one occasion!

On 23rd June 1944, an Allied Pilot Training Course for 17 Poles, 2 Czechs, 2 French and 1 Belgian also started training. Then following the success of this course 22 Officers and 22 NCO Canadian pilots commenced further flying training with No.16 (P) SFTS.

Despite the intense training programme, many found time to explore the surrounding area or head off into Nottingham to practice their English on the local girls. *"The Black Boy was the pub for us, although we sometimes went to the George or The Flying Horse"* explains Ted Shuvalski; *"Although the war was going on, the attitude of young people was that we were not worried about it. We just tried to enjoy it as much as we could".* He eventually went on to meet his first wife at Newton, a Polish WAAF and got married in the stations Roman Catholic chapel. While Aleksander Gertner met his English wife during a trip to the Palais de Dance, others were to meet at the Astoria and Victoria Ballrooms.

By the end of the war, 42 of the 1525 Polish airmen trained at Newton had received British decorations in their fight to liberate Europe. These consisted of 1 OBE, 1 DSO, 21 DFCs, 12 DFMs, 6 AFCs and 1 AFM, often decorated by the exiled Polish premier, General Sikorski. For those who died a huge cross commemorates their sacrifice in the Polish cemetery at Newark. Sikorski was also laid to rest here, before his body was flown home to Poland after the collapse of communism. The cross has twelve badges of Polish Squadrons and the words of St Paul:

I HAVE FOUGHT A GOOD FIGHT,
I HAVE FINISHED MY COURSE,
I HAVE KEPT THE FAITH.

But in the end a lot of them felt that there was no victory as Poland was 'sold out' to Stalin. The Polish servicemen who not did return 'home' to suffer the communist regime, remained in and around Nottingham to establish a large Polish community. Ted Shuvalski remained in the RAF, flying Lincolns with 97 Sqn before converting to Dragonfly and Whirlwind helicopters, which he flew with 194 Sqn in Malaya and Borneo. During 1954 he was one of several pilots chosen to fly Lancasters during the filming of 'The DamBusters', which was no doubt helped by the reputation amongst Polish aircrew for low flying. Such flying would come in useful during filming over the Lake District and Derwent dam. After travelling the world with them for 22 years he returned to Nottingham after his first wife died as the lively city also reminded him of his home town of Lwów in Poland, now in Ukraine and renamed L'viv. While his friend Aleksander Gertner never moved away and joined the Polish Resettlement Corps in the City. By the mid 1950s the Polish Air Force Association had acquired premises on Pelham Road off Sherwood Rise in Nottingham and set up a lasting tie with Newton, which had earned the nickname of 'Little Poland'.

Right: **A wartime Battery House near the old windmill, 1998.** M & D Sibley

Below: **RAF Fitter 2E (Engines), Lewin Grant.** Margaret Grant collection

Above: **The Pratt & Whitney R-985-AN6 Wasp Junior radial piston engine on the Airspeed Oxford.** T O'Brien

Below: **Miles Master III, W8931 '30', being prepared for a flight at Newton, 1943.** A Choloniewski

Crunch!

Left and below: **Airspeed Oxford NM420** that crashed on the edge of the airfield at 22.50 hours on 16th March 1945 killing Flt Lt Sadowski (Nav Instructor) and Lieut. Piotrowski (Pupil). Only W O Ballard (Wireless Operator) survived.
Charles Waterfall collection

Bottom: **Miles Master II, DL938** that came to grief following an air-test on 25th March 1944 near the old derelict windmill, which can be seen still standing in the top left of the photograph. Pilot Officer Szwede (Flying Instructor) and his passenger, Sgt Brown of the servicing flight were both killed instantly.
Charles Waterfall collection

Top Secret!

'Top Barn' sits literally at the top end of the eastern edge of the airfield near Oatfield Lane. Today, leased from the Crown Estate by farmer, Roger Miller of Shelford, it is now home to the Shelford Gun Club. But in wartime was used as a top secret wireless school with an English instructor, Henry Clough, to teach Polish students how to communicate over the radio in English. Jan Krupa remembers the secretive barn as it was always 'out of bounds' during the war. In the 1980s, the barn was requisitioned again on several occasions when Roger Miller was asked not to use the barn for a few days as the Police Dogs needed it as a sterile training area. Photograph by T.O'Brien.

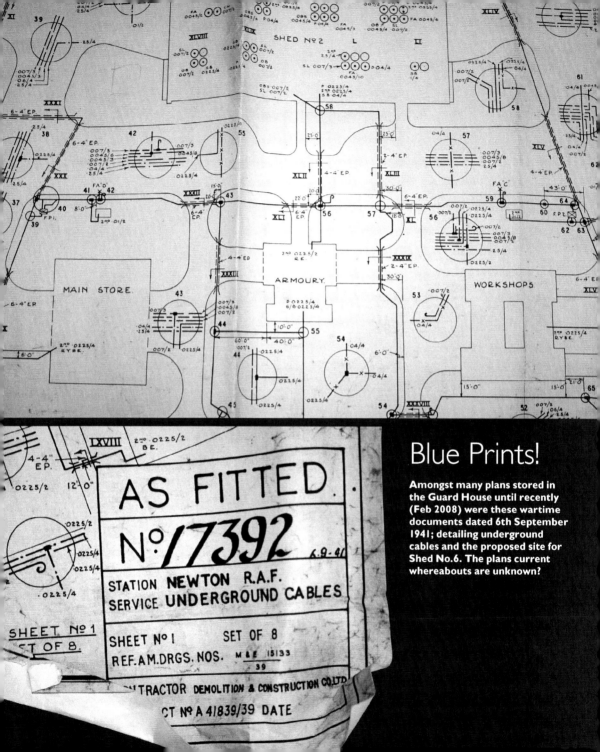

Blue Prints!

Amongst many plans stored in the Guard House until recently (Feb 2008) were these wartime documents dated 6th September 1941; detailing underground cables and the proposed site for Shed No.6. The plans current whereabouts are unknown?

Left: **An interior view of the Decontamination centre.** T O'Brien

Below left: **The Decontamination showers.** T O'Brien

Far left: **The ground floor machinery inside the Water Tower.** T O'Brien

Bottom: **A panoramic shot of the Water Tower and Decontamination Centre, February 2008.** Adam Davey

Station Buildings

Top left: **Building 17, a 4 Bay Petrol Tanker Shed.**
J Proudlock

Above left: **Fire Tender Shed next to the Tower**
J Proudlock

Top right: **Building 43, the wartime Ration store and Post-war catering flight.** T O'Brien

Above right: **The Supply Squadron, late 1970s.**
Richard Harcourt

Top left: **Building 31, the Lubricants and Inflammable Oils store.** T O'Brien

Top right: **Building 37a, the wartime Disinfector Boiler House or Laundry.** J Proudlock

Above left: **The PSA staff building that was constructed in the mid-1980s replacing a wartime hut that came from Swinderby.** T O'Brien

Above right: **Building 95, A Pyrotechnic Store** J Proudlock

Below: **A panorama looking north from 5 Hangar across to the former Supply Flight building. Note how the metal doors have been removed.** Adam Davey

'Newton Approach'

Landing chart information: **EGXN. Airfield Elevation = 182ft. Runway 25/07 – 3700ft (1128m). Runway 01/19 – 2300ft (700m), Runway 13/31 – 2300ft (700m). Runways marked on one side only by 25ft long white painted inlaid concrete strips at 100ft intervals. The active runway is marked by four frangible DayGlo red and white marker boards positioned on both sides of the threshold. The holding point is marked by a frangible yellow cube bearing a black 'M'. Newton retains a signal square bi-gram 'NW'.**

The photograph was taken in the late 1980s from a Chipmunk of 7AEF. Note the clarity of the grass runways compared to the 2008 photos elsewhere in this book.

The funeral procession of three dead airmen; outside the Sick Quarters; en-route to the Catholic Church. J Warchal collection

Jozef Warchal (centre) and fellow pilots at Newton. J Warchal collection

I Will Survive!

Harvard FT375, one of the aircraft flown by No.16 (Polish) Flying Training School is incredibly still flying today. But its career almost ended prematurely following a mid-air collision in 1945.

At 1105 hours on 21st April 1945 it took off from the school's satellite station at Tollerton as part of a *Vic* formation of three aircraft. Instructor, Flying Officer Podbereski was in the lead aircraft, Harvard FX260, pupil AC2 Salwa was No.2 solo in Harvard FT375 and AC2 Czarniecki was No.3 solo in Harvard KF366.

Having climbed to 6500 feet, the instructor entered a straight dive still in *Vic* formation. No.2 solo in FT375 found himself a little below and too far behind No.1 and tried to catch up. But as he was doing so, the lead aircraft began a climbing turn to the left and saw No.3 slightly above him and No.2 FT375 turning towards his starboard aileron. To avoid this danger, the lead Harvard broke away by pulling the nose up and right to take him above No.2 FT375. Meanwhile, No.3 KF366 became too close to FT375 and crunch, they both collided. Unfortunately KF366 came off worse as the rear tail portion separated from the fuselage, while the forward section with AC2 Czarniecki still inside plummeted to earth killing him instantly. While AC2 Salwa in FT375 only came away with a damaged tailplane, shattered cockpit hood and a dented panel before belly-landing back at Tollerton.

Harvard IIB, FT375 over the satellite station of Tollerton.
Artist – T O'Brien GAvA

Once repaired, FT375 continued to enjoy a very long military career with the Royal Air Force and ultimately served with Aeroplane & Armamant Experimental Establishment (A&AEE) at Boscombe Down, Wiltshire as a low speed camera-ship. It was sold by the MoD at auction in May 1996 registered G-BWWL to an Italian owner and continues to fly today around the skies of Palma.

Relief Landing Grounds

As the number of courses increased the pressure on the grass runways at Newton, Relief Landing Grounds or Satellite landing grounds were put into service.

Left: **An Avro Anson from Newton over the swing bridge at Sutton Bridge, Lincolnshire, 1944.**
Artist – T O'Brien GAvA

Below left and right: **Two remaining hardstandings on Bottesford Lane, Orston in December 2007. The 1,200 yard grass landing strip soon disappeared under the plough after the war.** T O'Brien

Bottom: **An Oxford passes the signal box at Bottesford West Junction while on approach to Orston, January 1945.** Artist – T O'Brien GAvA

Jozef's Long and Winding Road

Warrant Officer Jozef Warchal, like many Polish pilots travelled a long and winding road to reach England. Jozef, the youngest of six children, began his journey on 1st September 1932 when at sixteen he joined the Cadet Flying School at Bydgoszcz and learned to fly gliders. When Germany invaded seven years later, he was flying PZL.23 Karas light bombers. Four days into the German Blitzkrieg, Jozef's unit was ordered to fly south into Romania and collect Hurricane fighters sent by the British. But as they approached the border, their Karas ran out of fuel and they made a force landing. The three-man crew walked the final 12km to the Danube and waded across before being interned at Kampulunk.

Five weeks later, as news of the German advance spread; the guards fled. Jozef escaped along with four other pilots. Armed with money provided by British agents they bribed their way onto a train; then with the aid of the conductor, jumped off at Bucharest. Arriving at the Polish Embassy they were given false documents and rail passes to France. Their journey took them via Hungary, Yugoslavia and Italy before arriving in Lyons where they spent the next three months learning the French language in anticipation of flying with the French Air Force. After a transfer to Le Bourget near Paris; Jozef was then given an additional choice of flying with the British. Jumping at this he was soon on a boat.

Then, after flying Ansons with Coastal Command and Lysanders on Army Co-operation duties he was posted to 303 and later 308 Squadron; where he loved flying Hurricanes and Spitfires. On 16th April 1942 while flying Spitfire Vb, AB790 of 308 Sqn during a 'Rodeo' he suffered a Glycol leak at 32,000ft; the result of flak. With a wind-milling prop he trimmed the Spit and glided in a steep descent to crash land in Kent. Sustaining serious head injuries, he was stood-down from operational frontline duties; much to his frustration. After a short spell ferrying aircraft for Transport Command he was sent on an instructor course: then posted to Newton. But, the yearning to get back into a Spitfire cockpit remained.

While billeted at Newton Jozef flew the Master and Harvard from the satellite station at Tollerton. On one occasion he and his pupil crashed a Master following an engine failure. Both miraculously walked away unharmed. Jozef remembers the grass at Tollerton being ripe with mushrooms which they often harvested for cooking; while Newton provided rabbits and hares. He met his future wife, Georgina at the Palais de Danse in Nottingham and married in 1947 before settling in Gedling, Nottingham after his demob in 1949. The Warchal's eventually moved to Bilborough; another suburb where they grew and sold produce from their Aspley Lane allotment; which they enjoyed until retirement.

On Wednesday 3rd June 2009, 93 year-old Jozef, was finally reunited with his beloved Spitfire courtesy of the Battle of Britain Memorial Flight at Coningsby where he climbed into the cockpit of their Mark Vb. His journey had come full circle.

Photographs and memorabilia from
Jozef's photo albums, from the top:

**Jozef in the cockpit of Spitfire Vb,
AB910 of the BBMF, Coningsby;
June 2009.** Kathy Easter

**Jozef (93) and Georgina (89) in
April 2009.** T O'Brien

Jozef and Georgina; 1947.

**A formal wartime portrait of
Jozef in uniform.**

**A wartime flying clothing card
issued by the Equipment Section;
Newton.**

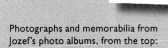

Form 667 B.

NAME WARCHAL J

RANK & No. 740527   P/O.

ROYAL AIR FORCE

FLYING CLOTHING CARD

Date of Issue
and
Unit Stamp

EQUIPMENT SECTION
19 JAN 1944
R.A.F. NEWTON

Signature of Accountant Officer
EQUIPMENT

Flying the Friendly Skies

On 8th May 1945 Germany surrendered to bring the War in Europe to a close, followed by Japan on 14th August after the dropping of the Atom bombs. In the aftermath of war it was obvious that Britain's huge Defence Budget had to be dramatically reduced to rescue the national economy that was close to collapse. As a consequence many squadrons were disbanded, aircraft scrapped and airfields closed. But the grass airfield at Newton survived and No.16 Flying Training School remained, where it continued to train a limited number of pilots with the remit to train 'sufficient Polish aircrew to maintain the existing forces at peacetime casualty rates'. Before the school was officially disbanded on 18th December 1946, Air Marshal Sir Arthur Cunningham KCB, Commander in Chief of Flying Training Command visited Newton on 9th September 1946 to say farewell to the Polish personnel who were soon to leave his command.

After a short spell under care and maintenance with only a small holding party in residence, Newton was transferred to Fighter Command in January 1947, when No.12 Group headquarters moved from its wartime home at Watnall, Nottinghamshire. During this period, they took over the station headquarters (building 61) and turned it into their Group HQ, while the station commander and station headquarters were based in the wartime armoury (building 27). The role of the Command, like Bomber Command was constantly changing and from its initial duty of defending the United Kingdom, by the mid 1950s was tasked with alerting, in the event of a crisis the V-Bombers and the defence of their bases 24 hours a day. Squadrons that came under 12 Group's command were stationed as far away as Aldergrove in Northern Ireland and those nearer like No.504 (County of Nottingham) Squadron of the Royal Auxillary Air Force at Wymeswold, Leicestershire. They were responsible for the defence of Eastern, Northern, Caledonian and the Western sectors of the UK. Whilst at Newton the Air Officer Commanding (AOC) of the group was at first Air Vice Marshal T C Trail before being succeeded by AVM G Harcourt-Smith then AVM Richard L Atcherley CB CBE AFC RAF and finally AVM W J Crisham. Of all these AVM Atcherley was the most colourful character. He was well known throughout the service for his pre war flying exploits along with his twin brother David, who was also a pilot in the RAF. Stories about the Atcherley twins are legendary, such as the time when one stood in for another at an annual medical examination or the occasion when one of the brothers inspected a parade by flying upside down along the front rank! Such antics didn't change at Newton, as he would often buzz the group headquarters at extreme low altitude in his personal Meteor 8. Once he 'borrowed' an RAF helicopter which resulted in papers flying off desks and out of the windows to litter the road below!

During this period some limited flying continued at Newton with No.12 Group Communications Flight that had also moved in, which was over the years equipped with an Avro Anson, two Airspeed Oxfords, two de Havilland (DH) Vampires, DH Chipmunk, three Gloster Meteors (one Mk7 and two Mk8s),

Top: **A Kirby Cadet III of No.49 Air Training Corps Gliding School over Newton House Farm during a summer evening, 1952. Kenneth Poxon who was a member of 138 Sqn ATC** remembers having several gliding trips from here during the weekends and evenings in 1949. He and fellow cadets also enjoyed exploring 58 MU's aircraft 'dump' on the far side of the airfield, where they found a range of fascinating salvaged wartime wrecks.
Artist – T O'Brien GAvA

Below: **A Percival Prentice of No.22 Flying Training School based at RAF Syerston** is seen over Saxondale Junction whilst coming in for some 'circuits and bumps' at Newton, 1950. Artist – T O'Brien GAvA

Former 7 AEF pilot, Reg Simpson at his home in 2002.
T O'Brien

Jim Elton by the tower in February 2008.
T O'Brien

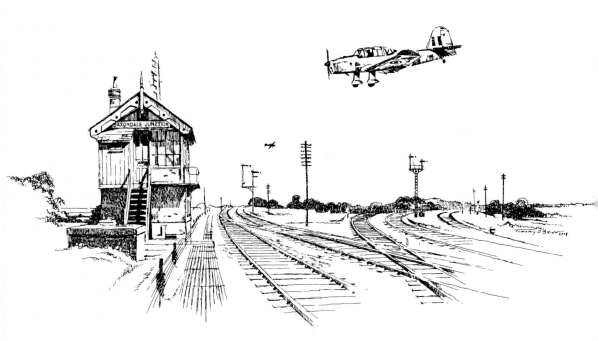

two Taylorcraft Austers, Percival Proctor, and a DC-3 Dakota. When the flight introduced the Meteor in the early 1950s, a steel mesh runway was buried under the grass surface for strength. Also the main 07/25 runway was extended from the 25 threshold to the rear of Fairway Crescent to create an incredible 'dogleg' bend or 'kink' of some 15 degrees, which would never have been sanctioned today. In July 1957, Meteor **969 made station history by being the aircraft to have flown the greatest distance from Newton. Flown by Gp Capt Morris DSO DFC it took off on 20th June bound for Tangmere then Takali via Istre. Sqn Ldr Smart MCN AFC then flew her on to El Adem and finally ending up in Nicosia, Cyprus.

As Newton was still under used at this time, No.22 Flying Training School based at RAF Syerston employed it as a Relief Landing Ground (RLG) between January 1948 and November 1951. Its naval student pilots would often perform 'circuits and bumps' in their Harvard and Prentice aircraft. Gliders of No.49 Air Training Corps Gliding School also used Newton during this period to provide glider flying instruction during evenings and weekends to local air cadets.

With the general rundown of the RAF after the war Newton received a few 'lodger' units. One was No.58 Maintenance Unit (MU) that had moved its headquarters from RAF Skellingthorpe, Lincolnshire in April 1947. Its function was the salvage and recovery of crashed wartime aircraft. In May 1950 the MU moved on to Sutton Bridge where they remained until being disbanded in 1958. For a short while Newton played host to No.9 and No.24 Mobile Dental Surgeries. The two units operated out of Newton between October 1947 and May 1948 to visit the large number of small RAF units that were still operating from satellite stations across Nottinghamshire and Lincolnshire. As wartime airfields began to close during the 1950s and 1960s, Newton also took on 'parenting' duties for these airfields during periods of Care and Maintenance such as Ancaster Malbis and Langar.

In May 1955, No.13 Group Fighter Command re-formed along with its communication flight which was based at Newton and consisted of three Meteor F.8s, an Anson Mk19 and one Chipmunk, so they could transit between Newton and the north-east.

On 8th January 1951, No.93 MU moved its headquarters in from RAF Wickenby with 40 officers and 1034 airmen on strength. With Group Captain L C Dennis as their Officer Commanding, the MU was responsible for the disposal of thousands of tons of bombs which had been stored at sub-sites on the disued airfields of Lincolnshire and Nottinghamshire. Their stock as of January 1951 was recorded as having 52682·5 tons of High Explosives, 12205·4 tons of Incendiaries and 325 rocket motors. Jim Elton remembers being posted to Newton in 1956 as a Corporal with 93 MU. As an Aeronautical Inspection Service (AIS) Inspector he used to work at the MU's explosive store at Bottesford airfield. Jim takes up the story, *Strangely enough Newton was the most accessible camp I'd been to, compared with Cottesmore and Swanton Morley. There was a regular bus service from the guardroom to Nottingham, so I seldom spent a night in! It was while I was at Newton that I met my wife Joyce. The*

Royal Observer Corps

Right: The cover of the souvenir programme to the 1950 ROC 'At Home' day which included aerial displays by Hornets, Meteor, Vampire, Spitfire, Tiger Moth and Sedburgh glider. Nearly 1000 members attended the day and were given short flights in an Anson, Valetta or Dominie. H F O'Neill collection

Below: The ROC on camp at Newton June / July 1964. An inspection is carried out by Air Vice Marshal J K Rotherham CB CBE BA. Note the Gloster Javelin of No.9 School of Technical Training in the background. Author's collection

Bottom: An earlier camp at Newton, 1957. Corps members are standing in front of the 12 Group HQ Communications Flight Vampire. Author's collection

ROYAL AIR FORCE, NEWTON

"AT HOME"

TO

ROYAL OBSERVER CORPS

11th JUNE, 1950

Souvenir Programme

FOREWORD

BY

AIR VICE-MARSHAL G. HARCOURT - SMITH,

C.B., C.B.E., M.V.O.

AIR OFFICER COMMANDING, No. 12 GROUP

"WE WELCOME you to Newton today, as members of an integral part of the widespread Fighter Command organisation and, more particularly, of that part which is closely associated with No. 12 Group. It is our intention, during the few hours that you will spend here as our guests, to demonstrate to you a representative selection of Service aircraft, both in the air and on the ground. At the same time, we hope that each of you will have the opportunity of making a short flight.

Personal contacts, of the nature of your visit today, are invaluable in maintaining and strengthening the firm bond between the Royal Air Force and the Royal Observer Corps, and it is with these thoughts in mind that we wish you a pleasant and entertaining day at Newton.

June, 1950   Air Vice-Marshal

headquarters for 93 MU was in one of the offices that ran alongside one of the hangars and I was billeted in the barrack block that overlooked the station sick quarters. I used to store my bike in the air raid shelter under the block. To get to it from the foyer you walked along the corridor, then opposite the toilets on the left there was a door just before the 'ironing room' that took you down into the shelter. Quite often though I would find my bicycle submerged in water as it was prone to flooding. Every morning we used to be picked up at the guardroom by a three-ton truck and taken out to the airfield at Bottesford. There were two giant crosses at each end of the runways to warn aircraft and the bombs were laid on huge carpets about 100 yards long across the tarmac. There were bombs as far as the eye could see. Occasionally we would take some of these bombs on the 'bomb train' to one of the 'laboratories' in an open ended Nissan hut to be inspected. I can also remember 93 MU having other sites at Fulbeck, South Witham and Ludford Magna. One night in every fortnight I used to have to be guard commander at Bottesford and one evening we had heavy snow and got stuck there with the guard for three nights!" Jim remained here at Newton until 1958 when he was posted to another station.

Following the closure of No.93 MU in the late 1950s, another unit soon arrived. This was No.6217 (Bomb Disposal) Flight of No.5131 (Bomb Disposal) Squadron, which had many flights at different airfields across the country, all tasked with the problem of removing unexploded wartime bombs (UXBs) from closed airfields and the surrounding countryside. No.6217 flight was formed at Newton for the specific task of making the counties of Lincolnshire and Nottinghamshire safe from wartime bombs. Their work also took them as far as Yorkshire where they cleared a former bombing range before it was handed back for civilian use. Now based at RAF Wittering, No.5131 (Bomb Disposal) Sqn continue to dispose of unexploded bombs and in 2002 were deployed to Kabul Airport, Afghanistan as part of the war on terror.

During this period of the domestic post-war front at Newton, building contractors handed over the sixth and final batch of Airmen's Married Quarters (AMQs) during August and September 1951. Along with the pre-war married quarters this now brought the total to over a hundred dwellings. Meanwhile at the other end of the station the Officers Married Quarters gate onto the A46 was presenting security problems as there were not enough station personnel to guard it twenty four hours a day.

By 1st May 1953 the station strength stood at 15 Officers and 414 Warrant Officers, Senior NCOs and other ranks. The WRAF element comprised of 2 Officers and 62 other ranks. During the same year, sixteen airmen and airwomen were selected to travel to London to line the route at the Coronation of Her Majesty Queen Elizabeth. However the year ended on a sad note for Newton as Avro Anson 19, VS507 of No.12 Group Communications Flight crashed on 4th December, whilst attempting to land during bad weather and low cloud. The pilot, Master Pilot J R Yearsley-Struthers aged 34 and five passengers returning from a sports event were killed with only one survivor. The pilot and two others are buried in nearby Bingham churchyard.

Barrack Blocks

Newton's large wartime H-Blocks were built to house 8 NCOs and 84 airmen.

A dormitory. T O'Brien

The communal washroom. T O'Brien

A foldaway ironing board. T O'Brien

A barrack block as seen in 1994. George Ward

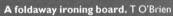

A H-Block on a cold February morning, 2008. Adam Davey

Two years later as the threat of attack by the IRA had increased the base took precautions in October 1955 by manning all the camp entrances and sending out extra security patrols especially around the bomb dump area. But during late September 1957 the IRA weren't the only threat as an influenza epidemic broke out on the station and lasted well into October, which affected nearly 200 service personnel putting a great strain on the bases operational capabilities. Then in late February 1958 Nottinghamshire received very heavy falls of snow, which totally disrupted the station. The snowfalls were so severe that station personnel worked continuously over a 48-hour period to keep the camp roads open.

1958 also saw the formation of No.7 Air Experience Flight, and under the command of its first Commanding Officer, Flt Lt Hector Taylor they flew de Havilland Chipmunks to give cadets of the Air Training Corps a chance to fly. A duty they performed at Newton until the airfield closed forty-two years later. One such pilot was Reg Simpson who was one of the original pilots to join the AEF. However for many he is best remembered as the England and Nottinghamshire cricketer, but had also been a Dakota pilot in India during the war. While he was recuperating in his garden in the late 1950s following a back problem, a Tiger Moth from nearby Tollerton aerodrome flew overhead. Not having flown since leaving the RAF eleven years earlier, the sight and sound of the biplane inspired him to take up flying again. Flying from Tollerton with the Chief Flying Instructor, who just happened to be Hector Taylor, he passed his Private Pilots Licence in November 1957. Then in 1960 Reg received an invitation from Hector to join the recently formed AEF. *"I enjoyed flying the cadets from Newton and teaching them to fly. Inevitably some froze as soon as they took the controls, but others were naturals at it and had a good feel for flying"*. Even though Reg's cricket days for Nottinghamshire were now over, he represented RAF Newton on one occasion during a cricket match played on the station cricket pitch. For twenty years Reg flew cadets of the Air Training Corps until his retirement in December 1980 at the age of 60 having amassed 600 hours with the AEF. But as a member of the Officer's Mess, he would often be seen visiting Newton until the airfield ultimately closed. A contemporary of Reg at the AEF was James Pickering AFC, who also had a distinguished wartime career as a former Battle of Britain pilot and went onto fly one of the three famous Gladiators 'Faith', 'Hope' and 'Charity' defending Malta. At Newton he also became well known flying his personal autogyro from Newton indulging in one of his pastimes of aerial photography of local archaeological sites during the late sixties and early seventies. In a strange coincidence his 'Wallis' autogyro G-ATTB had been built and supplied by Ken Wallis who had briefly flown Wellington bombers from Newton in 1941.

In 1947, another long term 'lodger' unit arrived at Newton. Nottingham University Air Squadron moved in from Hucknall under the control of No.64 Group with their five DH Tiger Moth aircraft. The unit was originally formed on 26th February 1941 and during the war years was engaged in the pre entry training of students for the Royal Air Force. The first Commanding Officer was an ex-First World War officer and member of the RAF Volunteer Reserve (RAFVR), Honorary Wing Commander C M Attlee, Professor of Education at University

Battle of Britain

"AT HOME"

2 p.m. on Saturday, 17th September, 1949

AT

ROYAL AIR FORCE STATION
NEWTON

You are cordially invited to join the Royal Air Force at Newton on Saturday, 17th September, 1949, and witness a Spectacular Air Display to commemorate the "Battle of Britain."

You are assured of a most interesting and entertaining afternoon.

ATTRACTIONS INCLUDE

1. Formation Aerobatics by Fighter Command's own Jet Aerobatic Team.

2. Formation Flying by No. 504 (City of Nottingham) Auxiliary Air Force Fighter Squadron.

3. Mock Defence of Newton Aerodrome by the latest Mobile Anti-Aircraft Guns against Ground Straffing Hornet Aircraft.

4. Dive Dombing.

5. Fire Fighting.

6. Crazy Flying.

— And Many Other Interesting Flying Demonstrations —

The latest FIGHTER, BOMBER and TRANSPORT AIRCRAFT and EQUIPMENT will also be on Show.

THE STAR ATTRACTION

will be the

HIGH-SPEED AIR RACE

which will include the latest and fastest JET AIRCRAFT in service, plus a host of other machines. Many ex-Battle of Britain Fighter Pilots will be among those taking part in the Race.

This Race has been Handicapped by the same team who did such a wonderful job handicapping the King's Cup Air Race at Elmden this year, and should prove an outstanding success.

JOY RIDES

are being provided by TRENT VALLEY AVIATION, and include FREE TRIPS for LUCKY PROGRAMME HOLDERS.

ADMISSION IS FREE

SPECIAL BUSES HAVE BEEN ARRANGED.

REFRESHMENTS AVAILABLE.   CAR PARK 2/-.

College, Nottingham. On 16th July 1941, RAF Newton assumed parenting responsibilities for the squadron, which was to start the unit's long association with the base. Despite being based at Hucknall, the squadron's first aircraft was a solitary Tiger Moth, which began flying from Newton during December 1941 in an air experience role for those under graduates in pre-entry training prior to operational service. Even though this situation lasted until early 1946, some 216 members entered the Royal Air Force as aircrew, 19 into the Fleet air Arm and 15 to the Technical branch. Flying instruction began in September 1945 and in 1947 with the reintroduction of the Royal Air Force Reserve resulted in the total number of aircraft increasing to five Tiger Moths. In February 1947, HRH King George VI granted the squadron its own badge. The central part of the design features a 'quiver of arrows', which not only emphasizes the association with Nottingham and Robin Hood but is symbolic of the squadron motto 'Strength in Reserve'. During the late 1940s the squadron flew two Oxford aircraft and a 'borrowed' Harvard from White Waltham during the early 1950s. The Tiger Moths were replaced in 1951, by DH Chipmunks, and in turn by Scottish Aviation Bulldogs in 1974. In 1967 it was renamed East Midlands Universities Air Squadron (EMUAS) in recognition of the recruitment of cadets from the Universities of Loughborough, Leicester and Nottingham. When not flying with the UAS, many of these students studied a range of courses from Art to Mechanical Engineering.

The squadron consisted of five Qualified Flying Instructors (QFIs) and a small administrative staff based at the units 'Town Headquarters' on Broadgate, Beeston near the University, although it relied heavily upon RAF Newton for a number of functions and the airfield facilities. Flying training during term time took place from Wednesdays to Sundays for Volunteer Reserve undergraduates who, although not committed to a flying career usually do apply to join the RAF. The squadron offered students a two-year course consisting of 60 flying hours and also offered training and administration for University Cadets reading for degrees prior to entering full time commissioned service via the Royal Air Force College at Cranwell. As I walk past the deserted annexe building alongside hangar No.2 I notice the abandoned UAS and AEF crew rooms, which takes me back nearly twenty years. I first came into contact with the UAS myself at the age of fourteen whilst I was in the Air Training Corps. I had won a Christmas card competition run by the Air Cadet newspaper and the prize was a flight in a Bulldog, which was deemed as something special as we only normally flew in Chipmunks. So on 18th May 1984, a hazy summer day I duly reported to the UAS as requested. Then after being supplied with a mug of tea by one of the university student pilots, I received a briefing from my pilot, instructor Flt Lt Phil Palmer who also explained that we would have to wait a while for the haze to lift. As the sky began to clear I knew that my day off school would not be wasted after all. As well as being able to fly in a Bulldog, I was looking forward to this flight as I had only flown for the first time six months earlier in a Chipmunk. Before too long we were looping the loop over the south Nottinghamshire countryside in Bulldog XX687, which seemed luxurious compared with the basic 'Chippy' as it had heaters, carpets and side-by-side seating.

12 Group Communications Flight

Top: **The flight's highly polished Dakota serves as a fine backdrop to the speech by the Secretary of State for Air, Mr Arthur Henderson as he opens the 1949 Battle of Britain 'At Home' day.** Author's collection

Right: **An Auster at the 1994 Battle of Britain 'At Home' day, similar to the one used by No.12 Group Communications Flight.** T O'Brien

Below: **Avro Anson C19.** Artist – T O'Brien

Opposite: **A Meteor and Vampire over the rail bridge on the A46 during the 1950 'At Home' day.** Artist – T O'Brien

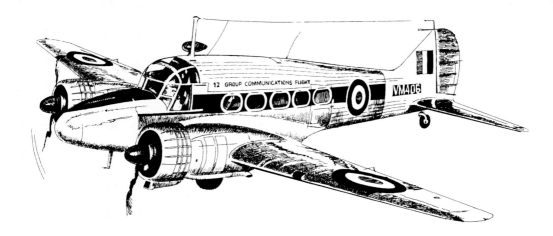

In 1991 I returned to the UAS on a professional basis when I was commissioned to paint their aircraft for their 50th Anniversary celebration, then again ten years later when asked to paint the aircraft over their new base at Cranwell. On that occasion I was also treated to a flight in their new aircraft, the Grob Tutor and invited to their 60th anniversary dining in night at the University of Nottingham on Friday 27th April 2001. Several founder members were on the guest list including Rt Hon Lord Merlyn-Rees PC MSc (Econ), the former Home Secretary and Secretary of State for Northern Ireland who flew with the squadron in 1941 whilst studying at Nottingham. During the evening, accompanied by music from an RAF band quartet, the Commanding Officer Sqn Ldr Simon Harcourt presented prizes and awards to squadron members. After the formalities of the dinner everyone headed back to the squadron's 'Town Headquarters' on Broadgate in Beeston, Nottingham to let off steam with a party. Some more unofficial prizes were then handed out before a game of 'Mess Rugger' kicked off the celebrations that continued into the early hours. As one of the last resident units to operate from Newton in the final 'detachment' years, several UAS students at the dinner talked about how they felt about leaving Newton in 2000. They all seemed to enjoy having the freedom of a whole station to themselves. Not only did they have their 'Town HQ' for socialising, but virtually had free reign of Newton's new 'Combined Mess' as well. Since moving to Cranwell though, a lot have now found that there is more going on and even more opportunities to party – it's a hard life being a student!

ROYAL AIR FORCE
NEWTON
MAIN GUARDROOM
ALL VISITORS
REPORT HERE
→

The Guardroom

Opposite page:

Top left: **Wooden Toilet sign.** T O'Brien

Top right: **1960s plastic sign.** T O'Brien

Centre: **The deserted Guard House in 2000.** J Proudlock

This page:

Above: **Faded signage in 2002.** J Proudlock

Right: **The main gate and lamp detail.** T O'Brien

Below: **A scene from February 2008.**
T O'Brien

'Strength in Reserve'

Nottingham UAS

Opposite page:

Top: **A trio of Chipmunks in formation during the mid 1960s.** EMUAS collection

Centre left: **Students practice starting up the Squadron's Tiger Moth, possibly at Hucknall circa 1946.** EMUAS collection

Bottom: **A student gives a Chipmunk a pre-flight external examination, 1966.** EMUAS collection

This page:

Top: **Chipmunks over Nottingham University, late 1950s.** EMUAS collection

Left: **Instructor and students during the final briefing.** EMUAS collection

East Midlands UAS

Opposite page:

Top: **A painting by the author, commissioned in 1991 by EMUAS for their 50th anniversary, featuring past aircraft over Nottingham University.**

Centre left: **A drawing by the author of the Town HQ on Broadgate, Beeston.**

Centre right: **Bulldog XX538, 'E', one of the first to be delivered in 1974.** EMUAS collection

Bottom left: **Students give their marks during the DH Trophy at Newton.** EMUAS collection

Bottom right: **Sqn Ldr Gregory's retirement.** EMUAS collection

This page:

Top: **A painting by the author to celebrate the Squadron's 60th Anniversary, the new aircraft, the Grob Tutor along with past aircraft such as the Bulldog, Chipmunk and Tiger Moth and their new home of RAF Cranwell.** T O'Brien GAvA

Below: **A Bulldog looks out at the grass runways.** T O'Brien

Mechanical Transport

The 'MT' section could be found in a number of locations.

Opposite page:

Top: **Seen in late 1999, Building No.7, a standard 'Expansion Period' Mechanical Transport Sheds, Office and Yard. Originally flat roofed. Roof added late 1970s.** J Proudlock

Centre left: **The MT Flight with their prize, 'The Company of Veteran Motorists Safe Driving Competition' Rose Bowl. Presented by Air Vice Marshal G L Seabrook CB FCA on 31st January 1966. The award was ultimately won three times in four years.** Author's collection

Centre right: **Presentation of the MT Efficiency Award to RAF Newton by the AOC No.24 Group on 12th June 1970.** Author's collection

Lower right: **Seen in 2002, the Car Wash in the former MT parking area outside No.1 Hangar.** T O'Brien

Bottom right: **Land Rovers in MT Yard, 2000.** J Proudlock

Bottom left: **Wartime MT Store. Post-war use as a motor club.** T O'Brien

This page:

Below: **Hangar No.1. Used by MT until to 1995.** J Proudlock

Bottom: **Building No.13. Wartime Articulated Trailer Shed, 2000.** J Proudlock

Above: **Desmond Penrose over Newton in the Arrow Active G-ABVE** on 14th April, 1998.
Artist – T O'Brien

Right: **DH Tiger Moth DE978 at Newton on 14th April 1948 after Desmond's first solo flight.**
D Penrose

The Quiver and Arrow

One of the student pilots who flew with Nottingham University Air Squadron was the well-known de Havilland test pilot, Desmond Penrose who has flown over 300 types of aircraft in his service and civilian careers. He is also known for displaying his 1932 Arrow Active MkII biplane for many years at the Shuttleworth Collection, Old Warden, Bedfordshire. Desmond tells me about the UAS and which aircraft he flew:

"I was at Loughborough College reading Aeronautical Engineering when I joined Nottingham UAS in November 1947. It was a happy, relaxed unit with very good wartime trained Officers and Senior NCOs. As for Newton itself, I have warm memories of the standard late 1930s Officers Mess where I could navigate, now, blindfold from ante-room to bar to bedroom. We were blessed with super civilian batmen, an age gone by. I first went solo in DH.82A Tiger Moth DE978 on 14th April 1948. Then during summer camp at Scone, Perth on 24th July 1950, I soloed on Harvard IIB KF691, which was a rare event for a UAS cadet pilot. Finally, when the DHC.1 Chipmunk joined the unit in 1951 I went solo in WD286 on 17th June 1951 after one hour's dual training. My instructor was Flt Lt Charlie Dalziel, a super chap who had a habit of undoing his straps and joystick, standing up, facing aft to hit me over the head with his joystick when I failed to carry out a slow roll to his satisfaction. He only stopped when, in exasperation, I started another roll while he was still un-strapped and facing me!"

Desmond won 'Best Cadet' during 1947/48 and was presented with the 'Jonathan Cash' trophy at the Squadron's annual Presentation Dinner in the Officers' Mess at Newton. He left the UAS in August 1951 when commissioned as a regular officer in the Royal Air Force. Later he attended the Empire Test Pilots School and at the invitation of John Cunningham, he resigned his permanent commission to join de Havilland as a Development Test Pilot.

On 14th April 1998 he returned to Newton, when he flew in his Arrow Active, G-ABVE to celebrate the 50th Anniversary of his first solo flight and by chance landed on the same grass runway he had flown from in 1948.

On the missile:

HM GOVTS HEALTH WARNING
UNTRAINED MISSILES CAN
SERIOUSLY DAMAGE YOUR
HEALTH

Four Hangar 'rocket men' with a humorous slogan, late 1970s.
Richard Harcourt

Rocket Men

Another roar from the crowd fills the hangar urging the vicious robots to exterminate each other during the production of 'Robot Wars'. Only the sound of the wind rustling the leaves on the surviving trees keep me company as I walk past No.4 hangar which used to house No.9 School of Technical Training's missile museum. Looking at the sad state of the base today it's hard to believe that Newton once played a vital part in the Cold War. Suddenly a tractor roars out of nowhere startling a few rabbits and birds before it disappears towards the grass airfield. As the wind continues to rush along the road, the distant echoes of the tractor appear again, bouncing off the hangar doors before fading away. Years ago it used to be the sounds of clanking tools, voices of service personnel, vehicles moving Bloodhound missiles into the school's hangar while Chipmunks chugged their way through the cloudscape above. Now it's more like the setting for a 1960s TV series such as 'Dr Who' or 'the Avengers'. I could almost picture the surreal scene in that episode where Steed walks amongst the silent buildings on an abandoned airfield, haunted by the sound of a mysterious milk float. The distant rumble of the tractor doesn't bother me though as I explore the base, but the prospect of meeting a renegade robot screeching 'exterminate' is a little un-nerving!

Following the use of atomic weapons in 1945, the world had changed forever and now faced the danger of nuclear annihilation. A new threat to global peace soon emerged, as the communist states drew their 'Iron Curtain' across Europe plunging east and west into a new 'Cold War'. To combat this, Britain and America started to build up their nuclear arsenals to act as a deterrent.

Newton was transferred to Fighter Command in January 1947 and like Bomber Command its role was constantly changing within this new world order and from its initial duty of defending the United Kingdom, by the mid 1950s was tasked with alerting, in the event of a crisis the V-Bombers as well as defending their bases 24 hours a day.

However the armed forces were to receive a devastating blow on 4th April 1957 with the publication of the White Paper *Defence – Outline of Future Policy* by the Defence Minister Duncan Sandys. This document restructured the whole future policy of Britain's air defence, deciding that there was no future in 'manned' aircraft and placed greater reliance on unmanned guided missiles in the defence of Britain.

A further White Paper in February 1958 announced the decision to equip Bomber Command with 60 'Thor' intercontinental ballistic missiles (ICBMs) purchased from America. From 1959 to 1963, Bomber Command's Thor force was maintained at constant readiness especially during the Cuban Missile Crisis of 1962 at stations from Norfolk to the Humber. Equipped with a two-megaton warhead and a range of 1750 miles these 'Leviathans' of mass destruction were divided amongst 20 Squadrons who had three each. Many of these units were ex-wartime bomber squadrons, including 150 Sqn that had been stationed at Newton with Vickers Wellingtons and was now at Carnaby in North Yorkshire.

In July 1958 'Bloodhound' surface-to-air missiles (SAMs) also went into service with Fighter Command to protect the V-bomber bases. The much improved Mk 2 version was then introduced with No.25 (SAM) Squadron in 1964 for overseas reinforcement. The Bloodhound was designed to intercept targets at a height between 10,000 feet and 60,000 feet at a range of up to 20 miles. To achieve this it was powered by two Thor ramjets along with four short-burning rocket motors that accelerated it up to a cruising speed of Mach 2.

With this greater emphasis on 'push button' warfare where humans seemed redundant, these policy changes started to affect Newton with the disbandment of No.504 (County of Nottingham) RauxAF Sqn at Syerston and HQ No.12 Group's departure for RAF Horsham St Faith, Norfolk, leaving Newton to be redeveloped for a ground-training role. On 1st October 1958, the base was transferred to Technical Training Command and became home to No.9 School of Technical Training (SoTT). A massive 'rebuilding' programme on the base followed to accommodate the new school, which was to become a world class 'Guided Weapon College' training personnel to work with the latest technology.

Around the same time, Lewin Grant who had been stationed here in 1944/45 as a Fitter 2E (engines) returned to Newton. But this time it was to be a brief visit as he was now working for the Cripps engineering company, who had a contract with the base to service various types of engines including one in the water tower. Lewin, couldn't fail to notice all the construction work in progress and seeing that part of the floor in No.4 hangar was being dug up, he asked the workmen what they were doing *"They are going to be underground bunkers"* came the reply. Whether it was a nuclear shelter or just channels for the underground pipes from the compressor engines in the annexe rooms isn't clear, but adds another interesting tale to the rumours about secret constructions and communication systems. Are they fact or just flights of fancy? Whatever the truth is, as there is no evidence to support their existence, they shall at present have to remain part of local mythology. However one story that is a definite fact is that the Royal Observer Corps held regular annual camps here at the time, practising their new role of alerting the country in case of nuclear attack.

No.9 SoTT was formed at RAF Yatesbury, an elderly hutted camp in Wiltshire and from the start it was destined that it be moved to Newton, where they initially operated from existing buildings while Four hangar was converted for the practical training on missiles. Guided Weapons Courses had been transferred from No.2 Radio School at Yatesbury by the end of 1959 and in 1961 they were ready to move into their hangar. In December 1961 a huge purpose built instructional block containing 22 classrooms, 10 laboratories, 2 workshops, libraries, offices and power plants came into use, initially for GW training. No.4 Hangar was also converted to include new classrooms and laboratories. The Station Commander, Wing Commander N F Searle commented at the time *"Of course we are still in an embryonic stage as a school. We are in the process of building on the foundations which have been laid – and literally building."* With the station now part of No.24 Group, the school was then presented with its own badge on 19th June 1962. In September 1962 two newly constructed barrack blocks were handed over in preparation for the predicted large intake of students. Extra houses in the married quarters had also been built, the airmen's mess extended and a brand new Sergeant's Mess was also constructed, although there were no plans to fire missiles from the base or build concrete runways on the grass strip.

As a consequence of these changes at Newton, the next few years were to see the base become very busy. From January 1960 to September 1964 the school was responsible for the training of servicing personnel for Bloodhound Mk1 and the Type 82 Search Radar and Type 83 Autofollow Radar, plus Blue Steel, Firestreak and Red Top missiles. In September 1964, the school expanded and took on the Electrical and Instrument Basic, Further and Post Graduate Training that had transferred from RAF Melksham. Courses were planned to last about 13 to 54 weeks, but as the vast field of guided weapons was developing at such a rapid pace the Senior Training Officer Wing Commander W Carmichael MA had to amend his syllabus almost every week! In the 1970s, foreign air force personnel from countries such as Singapore and Iran were also trained here.

Corporal Jim Elton had previously been posted to Newton from 1956 to 1958 with No.93 MU as an Aeronautical Inspection Service (AIS) Inspector. The MU was responsible for the disposal of thousands of tons of wartime bombs stored at sub-sites including nearby Bottesford airfield. In 1961 as the Berlin Wall went up, Jim returned to the station again as his trade had also been affected by these changes in defence policy. Jim remembers *"In 1961 the missile school had already got a few trainees on some courses, including myself. I spent twelve months here on a re-mustering course to convert me from 'Armourer' to 'Guided Missile Fitter'. We used to make wooden mock ups of the Bloodhound missile as part of the training and the school also had a transportable Type 87 radar that looked like a huge Darlek and a mobile Type 86 on top of a caravan for the Bloodhound system that were used out on the airfield."* These mobile sections were later to be deployed all over the world including trials in jungle and desert environments.

John Francis the General Manager the RAF Museum at Cosford also remembers Newton well. In July 1963 he was a Senior Aircraftsman and had returned from Cyprus to take up a new posting at Newton as a clerk in Station Headquarters (SHQ), where he was to meet his wife. John remembers *"In those days there was a nice family atmosphere in SHQ which is sadly lacking in a lot of workplaces today. Part of this community spirit were the cleaners Jim and Lal, who were a regular feature pushing their trolley around SHQ providing a terrific tea break service".* Amongst other stories he tells me *"I was based at Newton for a short time in the early sixties when the camp was settling into its new 'missile school' role. I recall that the day Kennedy was assassinated I had returned to the barrack block after work and heard the news over the station radio".* As well as the various missile courses on offer, John recalls that the base was also preparing personnel for the next generation of aircraft such as the TSR-2 that were due to enter service by offering senior management courses in the technical school block.

"In December the troubles flared up again in Cyprus and I was whisked away in the dead of night and sent back to Cyprus. However I returned to my job at Newton in June 1964. It was here that I met my wife Marie, who worked in the SHQ typing pool. In fact her whole family worked at Newton. Marie's sister was PA to the Station Commander, Group Captain Barber. While their father was a Warrant Officer and their mother worked in the Regional Printing Centre". When the Gardner family moved into a new house on Clumber Drive in Radcliffe-on-Trent John remembers *"walking or cycling down the country lane every night along with all the other servicemen who were courting local girls. On the return journey we all used to try and take the short cut across the airfield, trying not to get caught by the RAF Police"*.

During his brief posting to Newton, John became the organist in the station chapel, *"I also used to play the organ in St Peter's in East Bridgford and rang the bells at St Mary's in Radcliffe"*. In October 1964 John and Marie were married in St Mary's church before returning to Newton for the reception in the new 'Fosse Club', which was *"a great place for a reception"* he recalls. Shortly afterwards John was demobbed from the RAF and joined the Nottinghamshire County Police Force for two years until rejoining the RAF in 1966 to complete 24 years service.

Over the years the school used a variety of resources to help teach their students, such as 'redundant' aircraft types that were moved into No.2 hangar. Missiles would then be fitted to the aircraft and faults would be added by the instructors for the students to find by detaching it and correcting in the laboratory. The first aircraft arrived by road and were three Hawker Hunters WN901, WN904 and WV265. These were soon followed by English Electric Lightning F.1 XM187 of 111 Sqn and three ex-85 Sqn Gloster Javelins XJ116, XJ117 and XH972. In November 1969 a pair of Jet Provosts T.3s, XM402 and XM404 were also added to these training airframes. However not all the aircraft arrived by road as others actually flew in to land on the grass runways! Of all these arrivals the most dramatic entrance belongs to Avro Vulcan B.1 XA905 of 230 OCU that arrived on 14th September 1964, after circling the airfield a dozen times. The night before, hedgerows were ripped up in case it overshot the runway, but in the end it only went over by twenty feet and stopped well short of the field boundaries. It was then used in the Skybolt missile training system. Avro Shackleton MR.1A/T.4 WB849 flew in from St Mawgan on 30th July 1968 and was put to good use until replaced by Shackleton MR.3 WR990 of 120 Sqn that flew in during October 1970. Followed by Vickers Varsity T.1 WL637 nine days later and BAC Canberra B(I).8 XM271 of 16 Sqn in July 1972. All of them destined never to fly out again, as the runways were too short.

In part of Four hangar, the school also started from the outset to build up a collection of historic weapons that was to turn into a unique 'missile museum' which opened in 1963. Apart from the historical aspect, it was also a valuable instructional aid for the students, although members of the public were occasionally allowed in by prior appointment. The weapons on show dated from the rocket pioneers of 1943 with early German weapons through to the 1960s Skybolt, Thor and Blue Steel missiles of Britain's early nuclear arsenal.

During a visit, people were also able to see how an air to air missile actually worked, with the help of a 30 foot long electronically operated model on a display panel. It showed how a missile was released from a Lightning to seek out the heat generated by the enemy's engines before locking on for the 'kill'. To add a bit of light relief, a model of the unfortunate pilot was then hurled out of his cockpit so spectators could see him travelling upwards with his 'angel's' wings on! *"The school kids love that bit"* said Flt Lt George Duffill who was in charge of the museum during the early 1970s. This display was first demonstrated to the public during the 1972 Battle of Britain 'Air Day' at Biggin Hill and continued to be loaned out to other stations for open days and airshows.

But the writing was on the wall for the 'rocket men' following the RAF's restructuring policies of the 1960s and 1970s. Early in 1973 a decision was made to disband No.9 SoTT, with all electrical and instrument training being transferred to RAF Halton and RAF Cosford by the September. Airframes such as the Vulcan and Shackleton were then moved out and unceremoniously scrapped on the airfield. This just left the Guided Weapons Courses and Bloodhound Missile System Maintenance School, which were absorbed into the Engineering Training and Support Squadron in 1974 when No.9 SoTT ceased to exist.

As the world moved into the 1980s, the 'Cold War' and TV series' like 'Dr Who' still lingered on, as did elements of the missile days at Newton. If you ever visited the base during one of the Open Days you may well have had the chance to see the missile museum and sit in the cockpit of the engineless English Electric Lightning T.5 XS451, which spent many years being used for missile loading training in No.4 hangar before being demobbed in 1987, when the Guided Weapons Courses ended. She was subsequently restored to flying condition as G-LTNG before departing for Cape Town, South Africa. At the same time the 'Blue Steel' weapon departed for Newark Air Museum, while the rest of the missile collection was transferred to the RAF Museum's Aerospace collection at Cosford in Shropshire, where they now form a major part of the new 'Cold War' exhibition. By the end of the decade the winds of change were blowing again as the Berlin Wall was torn down, 'Dr Who' was axed and the days of the 'rocket men' at Newton were over. Walking past the awesome German V2 rocket at Cosford, John Francis stops and looks at the Thor missile towering above us and notes that; *"When I think about it, I suppose it is a strange coincidence that forty years ago I was based at Newton which was home to the Missile School and Museum and now I am looking after the same collection on behalf of the nation"*.

"I spent twelve months here on a re-mustering course to convert me from Armourer to Guided Missile Fitter."

Construction

Above: **The symbol featured in the school's badge.**

Right: **The huge technical block under construction on 22nd April 1961.** Author's collection

Lower right: **The completed technical block, 1st December 1961.** Author's collection

Far top right: **The wooden floors being laid in the technical block, 25th May 1961.** Author's collection

Far lower right: **The construction of new barrack blocks B & C, looking south 27th February 1962.** Author's collection

Bottom right: **The first Officers' Firestreak course, 26th January 1962.** Author's collection

Below: **Bulldogs of EMUAS are parked on the apron next to the Bloodhound missile and radar while a Chipmunk is on finals, 1982. Stories abound of how missile students supposedly used to track aircraft landing (totally unauthorised) to un-nerve aircrew and cadets!** J Proudlock

No.4 Hangar

Top right: **The interior classrooms taking shape during construction on 13th March 1961 with the steelwork and ceiling 90% finished. The radiant strip heaters have also been fixed to the roof metalwork. Note one of the air chambers of the Reavell SAT 7 compressors waiting to be fitted into one of the annexe rooms.**
Author's collection

Bottom right: **Dated 18th May 1961 this interior view details the internal classrooms, Numbers 24, 25, 26, 27, 28 and 29 nearing completion.**
Author's collection

Far right, top to bottom:

Exterior view of Four Hangar looking South-West in 2002. T O'Brien

An un-explained roof extension above the annexe rooms on the eastern side of 4 Hangar, which possibly housed an air conditioning unit. T O'Brien

1960s entrance porch addition to the western side of the hangar. T O'Brien

A Bloodhound being loaded onto a transporter, mid 1960s. Author's collection

Below: **Lightning T.5, XS451 during an open day, 1982.** J Proudlock

Mystery Machines

Today, sited in one of the annexe rooms on the eastern side of Four Hangar are several pieces of unexplained machinery. Asking several former personnel connected with 'Four Hangar', the author still has not solved the mystery, as no one was aware of their existence! But, the author's immediate reaction upon seeing them was that they looked like compressors of some kind. Further research with the original manufacturers, now called CompAir Reavell of Ipswich has confirmed that they are SAT7 compressors which was basically 1930s technology and produced by the company until 1980. They were slow running and reliable, which results in the company still receiving requests from past clients for spares! Unfortunately, that was all that could be provided as the original documents have now been lost or destroyed. If you know the answer, the author will be pleased to hear from you.

Left: **What appears to be an air filtration unit with a BIRLEC control panel and Moisture Adsorber.** T O'Brien

Above: **One of the three SAT7 high pressure compressors manufactured by Reavell & Co of Ipswich in 1961. What they powered is still a mystery, but could have been the power unit for test equipment, drills and other tools, which is the more likely conclusion or at the other extreme may have been for creating pure air to test the air-to-air missile systems.** T O'Brien

Boys and their Toys!

This page:

A painting by the author of the Bloodhound missile sited by the aircraft apron.
T O'Brien GAvA

Opposite page:

Top: **The missile museum, circa 1985.** Newton archives

Bottom left: **Personnel discussing manuals and using the Bloodhound test rig as part of the Guided Weapons Courses, circa 1978.** Richard Harcourt

Upper right: **The Station Commander, Gp Capt McTaggart, Wg Cdr I J S Corderey, OC Training Wing, Officers of 'A' Squadron and Singaporean Armed Forces and civilians under training on Bloodhound Mk2 courses, August 1971.** Author's collection

Lower right: **Royal Iranian Air Force students march past during the annual inspection of RAF Newton by the AOC No.24 Group, Air Vice Marshal C S Betts CBE, MA, RAF on 2nd May 1972.** Author's collection

On Parade

This page:

Air Marshal B Robinson CBE, RAF, Air Officer Commanding (AOC) No.24 Group takes the salute as four Chipmunks from Nottingham University Air Squadron fly in formation overhead, 13th June 1967. Author's collection

Opposite page:

Top: **The 1962 Air Officer Commanding's inspection of RAF Newton. Note the Astra cinema still standing between the Airmen's Mess and the H-Block shortly before demolition.** Author's collection

Centre: **Another view of the AOCs inspection parade on 13th June 1967.** Author's collection

Bottom: **A good turn out for a station parade in 1965.** Author's collection

Training Airframes

Opposite page:

Top four photos: **A sequence of photographs showing the arrival of Shackleton T.5, WB849 on 30th July 1968.** Author's collection

Bottom: **The crew of Shackleton MR.3, WR990 hand over the aircraft documents to Chief Technician David Carpenter and Flt Lt Humphries, TADO.** Author's collection

This page:

Top: **BAC Canberra B(1).8 XM271 of the recently disbanded 16 Squadron in Germany lands at Newton 26th June 1972.** Author's collection

Bottom: **Shackleton MR.3, WR990 of 120 Squadron lands at Newton, 17th October 1970.** Author's collection

'The Vulcan Landing!'

14th September 1964 was to become a landmark day in Newton's history, when 'V-Bomber', Avro Vulcan B.1 XA905 of 230 OCU from Finningley landed on the main 25/07 grass runway after circling the airfield a dozen times. It spent the next ten years in Hangar No.2 as an instructional airframe with No.9 School of Technical Training until being broken up early in 1974 out on the airfield. Lying on its belly after having its undercarriage blown off with explosives, the scrapman's torch was seen for miles around as they worked through the night to dismember this 'Cold War Warrior'.
Author's collection

"The night before, hedgerows were ripped out in case it overshot, but in the end stopped short by twenty feet!"

Retirement

At RAF Newton, when an Officer or senior NCO retired, there was a tradition to parade them around the station whilst sitting on top a 'borrowed' missile from the museum and see them off the premises by towing them out of the main gates. In later years after the demise of the missile museum, station commanders had an 'aircraft' float made by the University Air Squadron students.

Right: **Warrant Officer Burnett inspects station personnel at the guardroom, circa 1977 to 79.** Richard Harcourt

Below left: **Warrant Officer Burnett astride the Bloodhound missile as it passes the annexe to the station medical centre while being towed by a Land Rover.** Richard Harcourt

Below right: **An officer being towed by personnel through the main gates while riding the Skybolt missile! Late 1970s.** Richard Harcourt

"They always say that if the Government spends a lot of money on developing a military site, they must be considering its closure"

Winds of Change

They always say that if the government spends a lot of money on developing a military site, then they must be considering its closure. After the major rebuilding programme around 1960-62, Newton became the subject of such gossip in July 1967, when the Nottingham Evening Post ran an article based on rumours that the base may close down by the Christmas of that year. It had been confirmed that a survey was under way with the base's future in mind and that a decision could be made within three to four weeks. At the time there were 1200 service personnel working at the base. About half of these lived in the married quarters at Newton or at Whatton, Hucknall, Alvaston and Burton on the Wolds. Other married personnel lived off camp in private accommodation, mainly in Radcliffe-on-Trent and Bingham. In addition to this there were also 180 civilian personnel, mainly instructors and clerical staff plus employees from the Ministry of Public Works and Buildings and those employed by the NAAFI, all of which received a letter notifying them that their futures could be affected. Thankfully in the end Newton escaped and remained open, however these rumours were to keep reappearing to haunt the station for the next twenty-five years until it eventually became a reality.

Since the war, the British armed forces have been subject to a series of cuts and restructuring. This not only resulted in a general reduction of manpower and materials but in the geographical locations and global commitments. Through these trying times the RAF has always remembered the original theme of "*Quality before quantity*" as laid down by Hugh Trenchard, though this was often to prove difficult in reality. One of the biggest changes came on 1st April 1964 when the old Air Ministry ceased to exist and the Ministry of Defence was created in its place. In the cost cutting of the late sixties saw a major restructuring of the RAF. During April 1968, the RAF's fiftieth anniversary year saw Fighter and Bomber Command losing their separate identities to merge into the single Strike Command. Flying Training and Technical Training amalgamated into Training Command, followed in September 1973 by Maintenance Command being re-branded as Support Command to make the air force a much leaner service.

The mid 1970s were also to see a lot of changes at Newton, starting with the closure of No.9 School of Technical Training by early 1974. Then in November 1974, the School of Education, the Management Training Squadron, later to merge with the Support Command School of Civilian Management Training and the Air Cadet Training Centre (ACTC) all transferred from RAF Upwood, Huntingdonshire. At the beginning of 1982 the RAF School of Education became the RAF School of Education and Training Support (RAF SOETS) and subsequently absorbed into the RAF School of Management Training.

In September 1975 the RAF Police School arrived from RAF Debden, followed by the RAF Police Dog Training Flight. The Provost and Security Services (Northern Region) also moved in from Spitalgate near Grantham in March 1975. The autumn of 1975, saw the ATC Central Gliding School and No.644 Volunteer Gliding

School (VGS) move into nearby RAF Syerston, which was 'parented' by Newton, followed by Headquarters Air Cadets in November 1975, which moved up from RAF Brampton, Cambridgeshire into one of the 'H' blocks that looks out onto the parade square. In August 1977 the Air Cadet Gliding School detachment moved from RAF Swanton Morley, Norfolk when it amalgamated with its parent unit at RAF Syerston. Chipmunks from Newton would often fly over to Syerston to help tow some of the gliders and meals were often sent over in a Land Rover. At night some of the machinery including the winch launch was stored at Newton and on one occasion couldn't be used until a nesting bird had departed!

The next few years saw the base settle down into relative stability, with the resident units in August 1990 being: RAF School of Education & Training Support; RAF Police School and Dog Training Squadron, RAF Provost & Security Services (Northern Region); Regional Printing Centre; East Midlands Universities Air Squadron; No.7 Air Experience Flight; Headquarters Air Cadets; Air Cadet Training Centre; Headquarters East Midlands Wing and 1936 Squadron of the Air Training Corps.

An aerial view looking east, August 2008. T O'Brien

One of two history panels that used to be sited in Station Headquarters, but were saved from destruction or 'deep' storage by 1936 (Newton) Squadron, ATC when the station closed in 2001 both now hang in their headquarters, the old NAAFI shop. The panels were created in July 1974 by M D Rivers and R B Nicholls. Terrance Armson

ROYAL AIR FORCE NEWTON
1958 — 1975

On the 1st October 1958 Newton was taken over by Technical Training Command and following a rebuilding programme became officially known as No 9 School of Technical Training. From January 1960 to September 1964, 9 S of TT was responsible for the training of Servicing personnel for Bloodhound Mks 1 and 2, Blue Steel, Firestreak and Red Top missiles. In September 1964, 9 S of TT was expanded to absorb Electrical and Instrument Basic, Further and Post Graduate Training transferred from R A F Melksham.

In April 1970, the Freedom of the City of Nottingham was conferred upon the station. Early in 1975 a decision was taken to disband 9 S of TT. All Electrical and Instrument training was transferred to Halton and Cosford by September 1975 but Guided Weapon training was retained within an Engineering Training and Support Squadron. Many existing buildings were converted to accommodate redeployments to Newton following the closure of other R A F stations.

In November 1974 the R A F School of Education was transferred from Upwood and continued to provide training in Instructional Techniques, Management of Training, English Language for Overseas Students, and an Educational Advisory Service for the R A F. In addition the Management Training Squadron specialising in Officer and SNCO management training, and the Air Cadet Training Centre providing courses for R A F PR (T) Admin Officers and Warrant Officers, arrived from Upwood.

Also in November 1974 the R A F Police School arrived from Debden to continue with its task of training R A F Policemen and Policewomen. In March 1975 the R A F Provost and Security Services (Northern Region) arrived from Spitalgate, at the same time the R A F Central Gliding School and No 644 Gliding School moved to Syerston airfield for parenting by Newton.

Following the building of a dog training complex on the south west perimeter of the airfield, the R A F Police Dog Training Flight from Debden joined the R A F Police School in September 1975.

In November 1975, Headquarters Air Cadets arrived from Brampton and continued its task of administering the 42 Wings and 867 Squadrons of the Air Training Corps throughout the United Kingdom.

We Teach and We Learn

Leaving the car by the entrance of the large retro sixties building on my penultimate visit to Newton, I get out and start walking round the crumbling structure. The silence on this December day, 2007 is shattered as a bird flies out of a broken window to one of the classrooms of the old School of Education. It might even have been the very classroom I sat in one weekend during 1989, gazing at the view outside instead of paying attention to what was being taught on the ATC Cadet Warrant Officers course. Apart from the first year of operational service when bombers flew from the base, the rest of Newton's military career was devoted to training with units such as the Polish Flying Training School, the RAF Police School, Dog Training Squadron, the University Air Squadron and the Air Experience Flight.

In 1974, the School of Education established itself in the old technical training school educational block and for just over twenty years taught a range of disciplines in instructional techniques, management of training, English language for overseas students (ELOS) and provided an Educational Consultancy and Advisory Service for the RAF. In addition the Management Training Squadron specialised in Officer and Senior Non Commissioned Officers (SNCO) Management Training.

In March 2006, Officer Commanding of the School, the late Group Captain Roland Lloyd (Retd) told me that he had moved with the school from RAF Upwood, Huntingdonshire. He said that one of the first tasks was to clear the old laboratories of redundant equipment and turn them into classrooms. As the world changed, so did the school by adapting and growing to meet new challenges, which were also reflected in the title of the unit. By the late 1980s, the name had become the RAF School of Education and Training Support (SOETS). When the school was originally formed in 1948, its major role was the training of the air force's own education officers, but rapidly expanded into to the area of providing instructional techniques to train any personnel involved in training students. When interviewed in 1990 for the RAF News, Roland Lloyd explained, *"Over the years the RAF has changed its requirement in the fields of education and training and management training, so the school has also grown to meet them and now includes 'Training Support' in its title."* In 1992, the Department of Training moved in from Abingdon before merging in February 1993 creating yet another name change for the school, now called the Training Development and Support Unit (TDSU). The Department of Management Training then became part of Newton's station organisation and renamed the Management Training Wing.

Another part of the schools curriculum included a 'TV Familiarization Training Session' to teach students the techniques of television interviews. The school already used closed circuit television for teaching methods and feedback sessions but decided to extend this into an extra course as senior personnel are interviewed on TV from time to time. They were once referred to in 1975 by Frank Bough

Top: **The retro sixties architecture on the 'College of Knowledge'** T O'Brien

Above: **The main entrance as seen in 2002.** T O'Brien

Right: **Sqn Ldr Norman Randall interviews Gp Capt Roland Lloyd in a TV familirisation session in the school's own TV studio, 1990.**
Artist – T O'Brien GAvA

of BBC's 'Nationwide' as 'Television Charm Schools', who saw them as a way of giving RAF Officers a smooth television personality, enabling them to skate around awkward questions. In response Roland, then a Squadron Leader and his colleague Sqn Ldr Newby who ran the TV courses at the time denied this, saying that the intention was to promote sincerity and honesty in the strange unnatural environment of a studio, where you can easily get distracted by all the lights and monitors. *"You can't woffle and flannel on television"* said Roland, *"You have to really know what you are talking about. So much of your face fills the screen they can almost see what you are thinking."* The students were also advised how to sit correctly, overcome the giggles, how to react to a barrage of questions, the interviewer constantly interrupting and not to move until the director says so at the end. As it has been known for an interviewee to stand up in front of millions of viewers, wipe their brow and say, *"Thank God that's over."*

In July 2006, I spoke to Squadron Leader Norman Allen who was based at the School of Education from 1976 to 1980. Now living in France with his wife Ann, he remembers Roland Lloyd and the school. *"Roland or 'Roly' Lloyd as I used to call him; our paths crossed many times but it wasn't until I joined the School of Education in December 1975 that we actually served together. We were both Head of Departments: Roly had Resources Management (which included the TV studios) and I was a Pre-Structured Learning Consultant. Roly left SOETS in late 1977, being posted to HQ Training Command at RAF Brampton. I then lost touch with him as I decided to call it a day after 25 years. Subsequently Roly was promoted to Group Captain and eventually after a further tour in his new rank he arrived back at RAF Newton as OC SOETS, then finally retiring after a tour in RAF Germany. Strangely enough when back in the UK in January 2006, Ann and I stopped off in M&S in Nottingham for a coffee: who should be there but Roly and his wife Sheila! It was nice to meet them again."*

Norman then went on to remember his own tour of duty at Newton: *"Of all the Royal Air Force bases I've been posted to, I remember Newton as a pleasant station to work at and the School of Education's building was an excellent place to work in with all the different classrooms and offices. Mind you I spent four fifths of my time there 'on the road'. My job was to make provision of services to enable trainers, wherever and whoever they were, to produce a) instructor material and b) distance / self-learning material. When I was posted to Newton, it was a strange coincidence as my father visited the base several times during the war. His name was 'Darby' Allen, a Gunner 'T' in the Royal Navy and he was a mines and torpedo specialist in charge of a specialist crew posted to Bomber Command Area HQ. They used to prime sea mines for the Wellington bombers to drop on 'Gardening' operations. His area covered airfields as far away as Scampton and Waddington to those nearby like Bottesford, Langar, Syerston and Newton. On one occasion at Newton a Wellington crashed beyond the guardroom and my father and his crew had to carefully defuse the mines. Considering that it was a relatively small station, it was also a very diverse place with so many different units some being under direct command of the Station Commander while others were lodger units. In all, it was a very happy station with everyone at the different units willing to help each other. Very few people that I knew disliked being there".*

OCTOBER TWO-FIT

In contrast to the large School of Education, one of the lesser-known training units at Newton was the Air Cadet Training Centre (ACTC), which had their own HQ and classrooms in one of the hangars. With only two members of staff it claimed to be the smallest independent unit in the RAF according to an item in the RAF News during 1990. It was also claimed that the unit's dog also doubled as the adjutant as two civilian posts were vacant! Flight Lieutenant Mike Revel and Flight Sergeant Terry Kynaston trained all the volunteer RAF VR (T) Officers, adult Warrant Officers and Civilian Instructors who run the Air Training Corps (ATC) squadrons around the country and in overseas locations. The five-day courses provided many techniques and drill instruction for their ATC students.

Casting my memory back to when I attended the Cadet Warrant Officers course one weekend run by East Midlands Wing, although I didn't appreciate it at the time, we had excellent facilities to hand at Newton. All the classroom sessions took place in the School of Education block before marching over to ACTC based in the Police Training Flight's Hangar where we practiced drill instruction and those that had travelled from afar were able to stay in accommodation on site. Oh well, nothing lasts forever and as the pigeon returns to take up his window seat again I get back into the car and continue the nostalgia trip.

The bridge over the drain in Dawson's Plantation. T O'Brien

Don't Look a Gift Dog in the Mouth!

The RAF Policeman's eyes scrutinise my Form 3822 beneath the white cap and shiny black peak, while his colleague slides a wheeled mirror under my Dad's Ford Cortina. From their temporary concrete and sandbag fortification, RAF Regiment personnel observe my Dad as he walks back from the Guardroom after signing in. The year is 1984, and the IRA have just bombed the Grand Hotel in Brighton hence the heightened security state. Purpose of visit to Newton: to attend a parade night at the Air Training Corps. The first RAF Policemen were originally Royal Flying Corps (RFC) personnel employed on Camp Police duties at Halton and Blandford camps. Then on the 1st April 1918 when the Royal Air Force was formed, these personnel became the first members of the RAF Police. In 1919 the RAF Police School was created at RAF Halton in Buckinghamshire and remained here until 1937 before arriving at Newton in 1975 to make this their 'home' for twenty years, the longest period in their history.

Nicknamed 'Snoops' or 'Snowdrops' by other servicemen, they dealt with a mixture of offences committed by RAF personnel including thefts, drunkenness, assaults, forgery, desertion, using insubordinate language, absent without leave, false imprisonment and other disciplinary offences. With their white caps, white belt and gaiters they would also patrol Nottingham and Newark to keep law and order amongst military personnel. An extract from Newton's Courts Martial book reveals that on one occasion during World War Two a Corporal of the RAF Police was actually "struck with a fist in the face" by a Polish airman. Another Courts Martial dealt with a Flying Officer who was "Behaving in a scandalous manner, unbecoming the character of an Officer and a gentlemen". Amongst the punishments for those serving time in the guardroom, was being sent to help on the station pig farm. The station Courts Martial book also includes extracts of several cases when Polish airmen flew without permission or at low level, a reputation the Poles were later to use to good effect with their wartime and peacetime careers. A charge sheet for case No.21 on 20th March 1944 reads as follows:

> ... a member of the forces of a foreign power allied with His Majesty, being subject to the Air Force Act as an airman by virtue of the Allied Forces (Polish Air Force) Order 1941, made under Section 3 of the Allied Forces Act 1940 is charged with: When on active service being the pilot of one of His Majesty's aircraft, flying it at a height less than such height as was prescribed by a regulation issued under the authority of the Air Council, in that he at Royal Air Force Station Firbeck, on 29th January 1944 when pilot of His Majesty's aircraft Oxford No MP 452 improperly flew the said aircraft at a height of less than 100 feet.

> (Signed). S Cwynar G/Cpt,
> Officer Commanding,
> Polish personnel serving at Royal Air Force Station Newton.

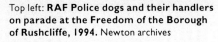

Top left: **RAF Police dogs and their handlers on parade at the Freedom of the Borough of Rushcliffe, 1994.** Newton archives

Above left: **An RAF Police dog warning sign by the main gate, 2002.** T O'Brien

Top right: **The 'sterile' dog training area behind Dawson's Plantation.** T O'Brien

Above right: **The interior dog kennels.** T O'Brien

Below: **The dog training headquarters.** T O'Brien

The RAF Police dogs were also a familiar sight around the station and certainly acted as an alarm system when a squad of air cadets marched past the kennel complex to reach the outdoor rifle range next door! But perhaps the public will remember them most for the exciting displays by their Dog Demonstration Team in the Royal Tournament at Earls Court, which is where they made their first public appearance in 1948. For their display, the Dog team thrilled the crowds with the routine of jumping through hoops and negotiating ladders and tightropes to retrieve items through burning obstacles. But when back at Newton they trained for the more serious task of detecting firearms, explosives and dangerous drugs. For this they used the training area behind the kennels and 'Dawson's Plantation', as was the long grassed 'sterile' areas on the airfields at both Newton and nearby Syerston. In the mid 1980s a training compound was also constructed within part of the old bomb dumps to act as a simulator in training personnel in how to guard weapon storage areas on airfields. Around the same time the fuselage of Comet C.2 (R) XK695 that had previously been exhibited at the Imperial War Museum, Duxford, but still on MoD charge was transferred to Newton for dog training.

Compared with the RAF Police, the dog section history only goes as far back as 1942, when the newly formed Ministry of Aircraft Production Guard Dog School was established as an economical measure to counter the threat of espionage and sabotage. This was the brainchild of Lieutenant Colonel (retd) J Y Baldwin, who in the First World War had observed the enemies use of German Shepherd dogs in not only guarding installations, but locating the wounded and pulling ammunition supplies around the battlefields of France. In 1946 it was renamed the RAF Police Dog Training School. The RAF Police Dog Demonstration Team also started to gain an excellent reputation during their public displays. This high profile also encouraged dog recruitment as members of the public donated German Shepherds as 'gift dogs' for patrol work or other breeds like Labradors, Spaniels, Pointers or any kind of Retriever or gun dog breed for search duties. After forty years of working with dogs, the 10,000th 'gift dog' entered service in October 1982.

The professionalism of the RAF Police Dogs, their handlers and kennel maids was soon noticed by other organisations. In April 1978 they were selected by Her Majesty's Commissioner of Customs and Excise to spearhead the training for a new national force of drug detection dogs to prevent illegal smuggling. They also undertook training of dogs and handlers from many other services and government departments including the Royal Navy, the United States Navy and Air Force. This reputation of expertise was also to spread overseas. As 'Glasnost' had started to ease tension between British and Soviet authorities, a special visit took place at the Dog Training School in September 1987. Greeted by the station commander Gp Capt Holliday, a dog owner himself, the First Deputy Chairman of Soviet State Customs Board & Council Ministers; Mr Vitaliy Konstantonovich Boyarov along with Lieutenant General Pankin of the Soviet Ministry of the Interior saw for themselves the work carried out by the Dangerous Drug Search Dog Cell.

The final display of the popular RAF Police dog demonstration team at the final Battle of Britain 'At Home' day, 1994.
Max Shortley

However the side-effects from this 'Cold War' thaw were the inevitable government defence cuts. This started on 1st April 1991, when the RAF Police Dog Training Squadron merged with the Royal Army Veterinary Corps to form the new Joint Service Defence Animal Centre and was to be located at Melton Mowbray, Leicestershire. Under the command of an Army officer and an RAF Provost Officer as his deputy the new unit was divided into two separate wings. The Army wing, which looked after the Army's horses and dogs remained at Melton, while the former RAF Police Dog Training Squadron now renamed the Dog Training Wing (Newton) of the Defence Animal Centre remained at RAF Newton.

But the air of change was to soon come round again when RAF Newton hosted the 37th and final RAF Police Dog trials in August 1994, before the station's planned closure. The event was filmed by the BBC for their 'East Midlands Today' programme watched by a live audience of 2000 members of the public. Another sad loss was the disbandment of the hugely popular RAF Police Dog Demonstration Team on 18th September 1994. Following this and the transfer of all dog training to the DAC at Melton Mowbray, the high public profile faded especially at events like the much loved Royal Tournament, which was also axed in 1999 after more than 120 years. By April 1995 the main RAF Police School had also departed Newton and returned to its birthplace at RAF Halton, bringing a close to another chapter in Newton's history.

"After forty years of working
with dogs, the 10,000th
'gift dog' entered service
in October 1982"

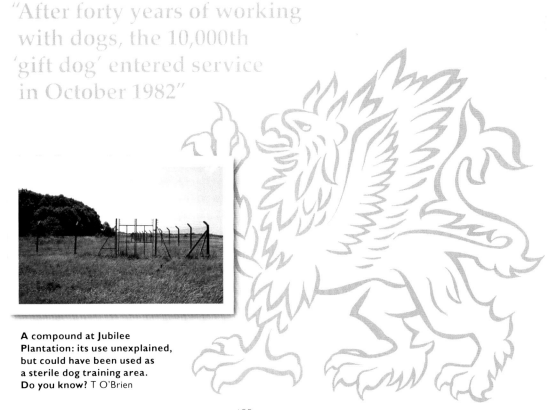

A compound at Jubilee
Plantation: its use unexplained,
but could have been used as
a sterile dog training area.
Do you know? T O'Brien

Bingham

RAF Police HQ
and Museum

An aerial view taken in
August 2008. T O'Brien

Newton
Village

A52

Lower Saxondale Village

Railway

Dawson's Plantation,
Dog Kennels and Training Area

Police Hangar

Police Training Flight

1936 (Newton) Squadron on parade for their 60th Anniversary celebrations in April 2002. T O'Brien

Venture Adventure

Standing in front of the two old wooden 'Spooner' huts that used to be occupied by the Air Training Corps I was transported back to when we all smartly stood to attention while they raised the flag before the evening activities commenced. On Wednesday nights we would march up to the hangars for drill sessions before heading back to the hut for lessons in airmanship, recognition, map reading etc. Then on Friday nights it was off up to the sports hangar or the shooting range. Crashing back to the cold January day in 2008 on what was to be my last visit to the station, the empty hut before me now looks tired and forlorn.

For many years Newton was associated with the Air Training Corps, as HQ Air Cadets, East Midlands Wing ATC and the Chipmunk aircraft of No.7 AEF have all been based there. But one resident unit that outlasted them all is 1936 Newton Squadron of the ATC, which was formed on 3rd April 1942 and is still operating at the former RAF base having witnessed all the changes at the site. Having all these other ATC units as neighbours could have its advantages for 1936 Sqn, but also restricted freedom in other ways. The most important neighbour was HQ Air Cadets, which had the overall responsibility for some 39,000 cadets aged 13 to 21 years in nearly 1000 ATC squadrons and detached flights across the country. They achieved this through 7 regional and 40 wing headquarters. The Air Training Corps (ATC) started life as a national organisation for boys called the Air Defence Cadet Corps, which was founded in 1938 by the Air League. The Secretary General of the League, Air Commodore Chamier then devised the motto 'Venture Adventure'. To meet the needs of a nation now at war, it was then formed into the Air Training Corps on 5th February 1941 by Royal Warrant to prepare many youngsters for aircrew and technical duties in the RAF and Fleet Air Arm. A new Royal Warrant was issued in 1947 to include training in citizenship, promotion of sport and adventure activities and the International Air Cadet Exchange Scheme got under way. In 1953, HRH Duke of Edinburgh became Air Commodore in Chief and continues in this role to the present day and in 1982, the Corps took the decision to accept female cadets.

Reputedly named after the first year that the Royal Air Force station at Newton was established, 1936 Squadron's first headquarters in April 1942 was inside the old Junior School on Bingham Road, Radcliffe-on-Trent. From here the squadron controlled four detached flights in Bingham, Bottesford, Lowdham and West Bridgford. Each flight met one night during the week then all paraded every Sunday at RAF Newton. Later on in 1942, they all transferred to Newton permanently to form one unit with more than 100 cadets parading in one of the hangar annexe rooms.

The first Commanding Officer was Flight Lieutenant Stanley Pritchard-Barrett who commanded the squadron from 1942 to 1944. He was a tall man, in his forties and employed as a local area representative for the Barnstone Cement Company in Barnstone. The company had been responsible for supplying the various contractors during Newton's construction four years earlier. Upon leaving 1936 Squadron he presented the unit with a large wooden propeller from an Avro 504N biplane complete with brass inscription plate. There have been many long serving members of staff, but Flt Lt John North survived them all when he retired from uniformed service with the corps in September 2002 after 34 years with the squadron. In 1974 he became the squadron's Commanding Officer before stepping down from the role in 1991 to become the squadron officer. Over the years John gave up a lot of his spare time away from his full time job as a teacher to help foster an interest in aviation and citizenship in others. He prefers to remember his time with the ATC as having *"served with many heroes and friends"*. One such person was Flt Lt Bob Truman DFC and as John remembers; *"Bob Truman who became the squadrons CO in 1967 to 1969 had won the Distinguished Flying Cross and also flew as an engineer in a 625 Sqn Lancaster on the infamous Nuremberg raid"*. It was to be the RAF's heaviest defeat of the war as 170 bombers were either destroyed or written off and 500 plus aircrew were killed during the cloudless night of March 30th 1944.

From the first annual camp at RAF Syerston in 1942, the squadron has visited many air bases including Coningsby, Leuchars and Northolt as well as Malta, Germany, Cyprus and Gibraltar. Transport to the UK locations was usually by coach from the guardroom. If the base had suitable types of aircraft based on site that could carry some extra passengers, then cadets often benefited from having a trip in something different, which made a change from the ubiquitous Chipmunk. One notable occasion was when the squadron visited RAF Lyneham in 1983. Virtually the whole camp went flying in a single C-130 Hercules transport aircraft. Everyone seemed to be enjoying the ride until the aircrew decided to indulge in some 'seat of the pants' flying, which resulted in several sick bags and one officers hat being used! One member of staff who attended that camp was Jim Elton, who had served with 93 MU in 1956 to 58, before returning to Newton as a Warrant Officer with 1936 Sqn where his son Steve was also a cadet.

By fostering the spirit of adventure, developing the qualities of leadership and good citizenship, 1936 Sqn cadets are also trained for civilian life as well. One well-known ex-cadet was Dennis 'Tug' Wilson, who was Nottingham's tallest Policeman at 6 foot 8 inches. In 1945 he joined the ATC after some encouragement from local cadets, as a goalkeeper was needed for the squadron football team! He used to cycle up to Newton from his home in Radcliffe-on-Trent until he left the Corps in 1947 to join the Grenadier Guards. In 1953, he was one of the guardsman who carried the coffin of King George VI. After the army, he joined Nottingham Constabulary to become a familiar sight patrolling Nottingham's Old Market Square. In the early 1980s at the Remembrance Day parade in the nearby village of Langar, 'Tug' Wilson was once again re-united with 1936 squadron who paraded alongside the Grenadier Guards Association, British Legion, Scouts and Brownies. Another cadet who went on to become a policeman was Mike Thornewill who served with 1936 Sqn from 1975 to 1980. Inspired by his time on the squadron working towards his Duke of Edinburgh award scheme, Mike and his wife Fiona from Thurgaton, Nottinghamshire gained fame in 2001 as the first married couple to walk to the North and South Poles.

1936 Sqn's immediate neighbours in the next wooden hut were East Midlands Wing, who moved in after East Midlands University Air Squadron relocated to No.2 Hangar. This replaced the old Nottingham Wing on 28th September 1972, and came under the responsibility of the North East Region whose headquarters were at Linton-on-Ouse in Yorkshire. Over the years, many characters have served the Air Training Corps at Newton, but one who sticks out in my mind was Wing Commander Ralph Reid-Buckle MBE, OC East Midlands Wing ATC. He would often drive around the base in his 'Silver Cloud' Rolls-Royce. He was also a member of The Leicester Aircraft Preservation Group that flew a Vickers Varsity T.1 WJ897/G-BDFT from Syerston and Newton. Unfortunately he came to an untimely end on Sunday 19th August 1984, when he perished along with ten fellow members of the group as the Varsity crashed into power lines at Marchington near Uttoxeter while en route to the Liverpool airshow. There were only three passengers who survived the burning wreck and all received serious injuries. I clearly remember that awful day as I was on my first annual camp at RAF Sealand, and the day before Wg Cdr Reid-Buckle had inspected the camp, promising to fly overhead on the Sunday as the camp photo 'shoot' was in progress. But that was last occasion the we saw him. The following week we formed a guard of honour at the funeral in his home village of Gotham, Notts. His widow then donated a large sum of money in order that a flying bursary could be initiated to allow cadets the opportunity to undertake a glider pilot's course. Wing Commander Berridge then took command, followed by Wg Cdr Philip Giles who continued to oversee the running of ATC squadrons in the local area until the Wing too became the victim of a restructuring programme and disbanded on 1st September 1999. Squadrons that had belonged to East Midlands Wing were then divided into Trent Wing and South and East Midlands Wing into which 1936 Sqn now belongs.

During the mid 1960s the squadron moved out of the hangar annexe and into a purpose built hut. Then in 1997 the squadron along with East Midlands Wing moved into 'Building 27', the old Regional Printing Centre. Then in 2001, the squadron moved yet again, this time into temporary accommodation (portakabins) pending the refurbishment of 'Building 127', the old NAAFI shop, which has become the squadron's present home.

Building 127, the former NAAFI shop, currently home to 1936 Sqn. T O'Brien

Top right: **1936 (Newton) Squadron on parade outside their 'Spooner' hut; Building 102.** T O'Brien

Right: **Building 27, the former Armoury and Regional Printing Centre and brief home to EM Wing and 1936 Sqn.** George Ward

Top left: **Building 149, the former home of Nottingham University Air Squadron and latterly East Midlands Wing.** T O'Brien

Left: **The entrance to HQ Air Cadets in 2002.** T O'Brien

Below: **A panoramic view of the parade square with the former H-Block and home to Headquarters Air Cadets on the left.** Adam Davey

TAKE OFF

with the Air Training Corps

THE Air Cadet

DECEMBER, 1984

AIR TRAINING CORPS

joins the fleet

The Air Cadet

THE JOURNAL OF AIR MINDED YOUTH

RAF Form 3822

T J O'BRIEN
1936 (NEWTON)
EAST MIDLANDS

Cadet's Name
Squadron
Wing

RECORD OF SERVICE

NEWTON SQUADRON
AIR TRAINING CORPS
1936
LOYALTY & ENDEAVOUR

JUNE 1989

Y OPENED

Cadet's Record of Service Book

E. BEDFORD
R.A.F. OUTFITTER
47 CASTLE GATE
NEWARK, NOTTS.
TELEPHONE—(0636) 703161

WE TEACH
AND
WE LEARN

Clean up campaign

BO

TRAINING

Opposite page:

Air Training Corps and RAF Newton memorabilia. T O'Brien

This page:

Left: **Flight Lieutenant John North RAFVR(T) in April 2002.** T O'Brien

Below: **1936 Squadron group photograph by the guardroom, 22nd July 1944.** 1936 Sqn collection

1936 (AIR TRAINING CORPS) SQDN. JULY 22 1944

Opposite page:

Top: **1936 Squadron on parade during the war, somewhere in Nottingham.** Geoff Miles / 1936 Sqn collection

Bottom: **Arthur Salisbury leads cadets of 1936 Sqn on parade past Southwell Minster, late 1940s.** Geoff Miles / 1936 Sqn collection

This page:

Top: **Air Cadets and airmen from RAF Newton on a wartime parade in Bingham.** Geoff Miles / 1936 Sqn collection

Centre: **Slingsby T.7 Kirby Cadet TX.1, VM528 of No.49 ATC Gliding School, Newton; November 1950.** L Hooton

Bottom: **Curious 1359 Sqn cadets inspect the school's first Slingsby T.21 Sedburgh TX.1 or 'Barge', November 1950.** L Hooton

Being the highest structure on the station, the water tower still dominates the landscape. Note the air-raid siren sited on the roof. When a practice alert was sounded during the cold-war, the slow wailing noise could be heard in neighbouring villages which could be a little unsettling! T O'Brien

History Repeating

They say that 'nothing is new' and that can certainly be said about history! Since the war, Newton has continued to become involved in national and international problems and bring them to this quiet part of Nottinghamshire. In January 1972 the station was put on standby to house the families of RAF personnel evacuated in the sudden British withdrawal from Malta. After flying into RAF Brize Norton, they then travelled by train arriving at Nottingham's Midland Station. Some were housed in married quarters at Hucknall, where a special unit from Newton, specifically set up to help the women and children settle in, had prepared warm beds and hot meals. Other families were housed at Syerston and Coddington near Newark, with the children being integrated into local schools. In the end, Newton itself was not used to house the evacuees and stood down from the crisis.

Since it closed in 1970, nearby RAF Syerston had been under the care of RAF Newton, until the 'parenting' responsibilities were taken over by Cranwell in 1995. In the early autumn of 1972, Syerston was very much in the news when it was announced that it was to be taken out of mothballs to receive 1000 Asian refugees from the former British Protectorate of Uganda that had gained independence in 1962. The Asians had been expelled from the East African state by military dictator Idi Amin, who then allocated their land and businesses to his 'political favourites'. Syerston was one of several RAF stations used to house the refugees as part of the government's 'Dispersal' policy until they could find new homes. Under this 'social engineering' plan the refugees were supposed to avoid areas such as London and Leicester that already had large ethnic populations. But despite Government attempts to spread them out, they still gravitated towards these areas to seek out family and friends. Officials from the Department of the Environment visited Syerston at the request of the Uganda resettlement board to give an opinion on its suitability as temporary refugee accommodation. As a result orders were made to prepare the site by repainting, cleaning and furnishing eight barrack blocks and the former airmen's mess as well as installing heating equipment. However, Syerston was not occupied in the end and stood down as Hemswell housed he refugees instead.

When Arthur Scargill called the miners out on a national strike in 1984, civil unrest was to come again to Nottinghamshire, reminiscent of the English Civil War. Violent confrontations often took place between the working miners that were being picketed by striking miners at the regions pits such as Cotgrave and Ollerton. This had all come about because of British Coal's closure programme of the nation's uneconomic pits. Traditionally the coal miners had been the highest paid industrial workers, which only strengthened the National Union of Miners (NUM) power. Over the years they had been able to call national strikes over pay and conditions, which quickly brought the country to a standstill as electricity supplies dried up as coal fired power stations were forced to shut down. The last major strike had also humiliated Edward Heath's Conservative government in the early 1970s. But this time Mrs Thatcher's government was prepared for what was to turn into a prolonged, bitter fight and this time she was determined to crush the might

Three Hangar, 2002. T O'Brien

of the unions. Power stations stockpiled coal and the civilian Police were called
upon to restore law and order. Due to the vast numbers of civilian police brought
in from around the UK, Newton's sports hangar was turned into temporary
accommodation for them. Rows of police vehicles with mesh covered windows
were also a feature of the station. The police were mainly called out to the many
coal fired power stations along the River Trent that were receiving local coal and
had been found out by 'Flying Pickets' from the NUM stronghold of Yorkshire.

As the dispute wore on everyone at Newton was eventually glad to see the strike
come to an end and life return to normal as the situation had started to cause its
own tensions within the base due to the loss of the sports facilities and the vast
amounts of overtime earned by the RAF Policemen's civilian counterparts. In the
end though, Cotgrave colliery fell victim to government policy in the decimation
of the United Kingdom's mining industry and had closed by 1993.

A Chipmunk over Cotgrave colliery, 1985. Artist – T O'Brien

An aerial view taken on 8th August, 2008.
T O'Brien

The Last Post

The constant threat of shrinking budgets eventually caught up with Newton in 1994 as it was confirmed that the base had joined the likes of Swanton Morley, Finningley and Scampton on the closure list, however it did not fully close as the airfield remained open and become an 'enclave' or detachment of RAFC Cranwell who assumed administrative responsibility for both Newton and Syerston on 1st April 1995. The night before, Newton marked its impending change of status with a sunset ceremony and farewell dining-in night in the Officers' Mess. During the ceremony the Station Commander, Gp Capt 'Sid' Adcock took the salute as the RAF ensign was lowered by an armed escort drawn from station personnel, while the RAF College Band played an evening hymn and the emotionally charged Last Post. Guests included the Lord Lieutenant of Nottinghamshire, the Lord Mayor of Nottingham and Mayor of Rushcliffe, the Provost Marshal, AOC Air Cadets, the Deputy Commandant of the RAF College Cranwell, the Commandant of the Defence Animal Centre, two former Station Commanders and the Chairman of the Polish Air Force 'White Eagle' Club in Nottingham. This also provided a final opportunity for the AOC Training Group; Air Vice Marshal J A G May to speak to Newton's personnel before many of the training units left as part of the Ground Training Rationalisation and Relocation programme.

During the following summer months of 1995, all the station buildings, billets and married quarters were cleared of their contents. I still have a vivid memory of seeing No.3 hangar being filled with furniture. There were stacks of 1940s Lloyd Loom wash baskets, tables, desks, chairs, cupboards, all piled up ready for disposal. The Hawker Hunter gate guardian had also gone. The Officers and Airmen's Mess had closed down to be replaced by a new 'Combined Mess' housed in the Sergeant's Mess. Slowly everything was disappearing until the station had become a deserted 'ghost town' by the end of the year. However EMUAS and 7 AEF kept the airfield alive. Then in 1997 some additional units arrived. They were the Slingsby Fireflies of the Joint Elementary Flying Training School (JEFTS), Army Grading section based at the newly re-opened RAF Barkston Heath just north of Grantham, who used Newton to escape Cranwell's congested airspace. No.73 Royal Engineer Squadron (TA) also moved in with its specialist heavy plant equipment. The Police 'Squirrel' Helicopter was also based here for a short while and carried out patrols of the Nottinghamshire and Derbyshire areas until a new site was prepared for it near Ripley. The Station Headquarters also reopened in October 1998 with Squadron Leader Colin Rawe as Detachment Commander.

While the rest of the camp started to decay like a ruined fortress, the married quarters outside the main gate were sold off to relieve the public's housing shortage, thus creating a new civilian community despite the lack of a shop or pub, just a small red post box! A fence was also constructed behind the officer's mess to cut off the officer's houses, as a new A46 road scheme threatened to obliterate this area. But the plans were eventually shelved – well for the time being anyway!

'Last Post at Newton'. A gouache painting by T O'Brien.

Hawker Hunter WT694 served as gate guardian from 1975 to 1995. A Chipmunk joins the circuit at he end of a days flying. The Hunter now resides at Caernarfon Air World, Wales. While the lagpole is enjoying retirement in the village of Westborough near Newark.

Then, in 2000 as the ultimate closure date drew closer the aircraft of EMUAS and 7 AEF then left their much loved grass runways during September for relocation to Cranwell and by October had fully moved their admin over. This was soon followed by JEFTS (Army Grading) who after a full day of flying on November 3rd packed their bags and on 6th and 7th November they moved out in several Pickford vans to their new home at Middle Wallop, Hants while the Navy and Air Force sections of the school remained at Barkston Heath, Lincs as the school had decided to split in two. The last of their Firefly aircraft took off from Newton's grass runways on Friday November 10th and the airfield fell silent. On Monday 27th November 2000 the final 'Last Post' was sounded when the Detachment Commander Squadron Leader Colin Rawe led a parade, which ended with the RAF ensign being lowered for the last time. It had been sixty years since the airfield had become an operational base. Amongst those who attended were Ted Shuvalski, Aleksander Gertner and other wartime aircrew, who had come to bid one last farewell to their old base. At precisely 3.30pm as Flight Sergeant Mick Issott lowered the ensign, a single Bulldog aircraft flown by Squadron leader Simon Harcourt of EMUAS made a poignant flypast over the ceremony.

The Control Tower then finally closed on Wednesday 29th November and all flying ceased over Newton. The Royal Engineers then started their relocation to North Luffenham and on 1st March 2001, RAF Newton officially closed and was handed over to the Ministry of Defence Estates Department for disposal. Plans were soon made by the borough council to build 3000 new homes on the site, which was thankfully halted when it was deemed that the local road and transport system was inadequate and in need of upgrading. With the closure of RAF Newton, the surrounding community had finally lost within a short time, the last of three large centres of employment, Saxondale Hospital (1902-1988), Cotgrave Colliery (1964-1993) and now RAF Newton, all gone but not forgotten.

A ticket to the 'We'll meet Again' farewell party held in the Sports Hangar, March 1995.

By kind permission of the Station Commander

Ticket
£2.00 per person

Dress: Casual

We'll Meet Again
Farewell to Newton Party
Thursday 16th March 1995

2000hrs In the Station Gymnasium

The metal boot-scraper at
the entrance to building 59,
the former Sergeant's Mess.
T O'Brien

Messing

The Officer's Mess, built in a Neo-Georgian style was located away from the main site in a more secluded area and has not altered much since it was first constructed apart from 'mock Georgian' double glazing replacing the old sash windows. Station Commander, Group Captain Philip Langrill recalls life at Newton's Officers' Mess. *"The Officers' Mess was active and well-run. The building was generally packed with both permanent staff and students and overflow accommodation was provided in various Officers' Married Quarters (OMQs). The length of many courses provided by our various schools varied, but they all tended to end on a Friday, which caused the preceding Thursday to be the farewell party night. These were often uninhibited affairs and I found it imprudent for the CO to appear in the Mess just then! We held regular dining-in nights and the customary formal receptions. On one occasion the guest of honour was Rushcliffe MP, Kenneth Clarke, who was then Secretary of State for Education".*

An insight into what life and changing social attitudes were like over a thirty-year period in the Officer's Mess is revealed in extracts from the 1955 to 1984 suggestions book instigated by the President of the Mess Committee (PMC).

The Fifties

18 July 1955   *"May I suggest in the absence of keys, some form of bolt or simple securing device be fitted to the bathroom doors. I am not unduly sensitive, but a bath would be more enjoyable if it could be taken without a succession of visitors!"*

23 November 1955 *"Each morning this week at 0600 hours, the loudspeakers in the Mess have boomed forth the Station 'Reveille' announcement. Suggested that steps be taken to prevent this entirely unnecessary and irritating practice forthwith".*

16 January 1958   *"Suggest that the Mess purchase a respectable coal scuttle for the ante-room, to replace the bucket at present used".*

26 February 1958 *"The BBC Television set is wonky".*

9 May 1958   *"Suggest the radiogram in the Ladies Room be serviced or replaced".*

25 May 1958   *"Suggest the piano be completely reconditioned and a contract placed for quarterly tuning".*

The Sixties

29 March 1960   *"Suggest that the piano in the Ladies Room should be tuned".*

1 April 1960   *"Would it be possible to have some fresh milk with coffee and cereals at breakfast instead of tinned?"*

20 August 1960   *"Suggest the 'Chocolate Chip Ice Cream' counter be removed from the bar forthwith and hid under the counter where it belongs! There is a NAAFI for this sort of thing!"*

16 April 1961	*"The highly polished surface on the rubber mats placed at the end of the table tennis table makes playing very difficult and could be dangerous".*
11 January 1962	*"Suggest an ash tray in telephone booth".*
11 August 1963	*"That a notice be displayed or that Sunday papers be stamped 'NOT TO BE TAKEN AWAY'. For three weekends running the popular newspapers i.e. Sunday Express, News of the world, People & Observer have been removed from the ante-room by 1900 hours. This also applies to periodicals".*
11 January 1964	*"Suggest that Officers living in married quarters should not remove the car washing hose and brush from the mess for use at their homes. Car washing facilities are provided at the mess for all officers".*
29 January 1965	*"I suggest that the dress regulations in Mess Rules be amended to allow living out members to use the bar on weekday evenings in sports jackets. This is done in some messes (Staff College, Bracknell for one) and removes at least one deterrent to 'popping across' to the Mess for a drink".*
22 July 1968	*"I find the taste of tobacco smoke objectionable whilst making a telephone call and suggest a 'No Smoking' notice be displayed in the telephone kiosk".*
25 April 1969	*"Might I suggest a change in the Mess magazines? Both 'Country Life' and 'Life' are little read expensive weekly periodicals and instead of them I should like to see 'Motor Sport', 'Yachting Monthly' and 'Amateur Photography'. Perhaps a vote could be organised amongst the Mess members?"*

The Seventies

20 February 1970	*"It is suggested that one feminine magazine be purchased for the female officers".*
14 February 1972	*"May I suggest that copies of 'She' and 'Cosmopolitan' be available in the range of magazines for the WRAF members of the Mess".*
8 April 1972	*"As an addition to the above suggestion, could the possibility of subscribing to the monthly magazine 'Hi-Fi News' and 'Record Review' be investigated on behalf of the Mess members".*
10 March 1977	*"I suggest that a duplicate set of keys be made available on the station for the Officers Mess bar, so that in the event that bar staff take THE set home, the bar is still able to function between 1800 and 2055 hours. This problem occurred last night".*
18 October 1977	*"That when one TV set is U/S (i.e. ITV), a serviceable set should not be locked up in the Locksley Room thereby reducing the numbers of available TVs to one".*
1 June 1978	*"That clothes hooks be provided in the bathrooms. The bathrooms in the West Wing (to the right) have no means at all for hanging clothes etc".*
29 June 1978	*"That the washing machine used on the upper floor of the West Wing (to the right) be either replaced with a quieter model or the present one overhauled to eliminate the 350 separate squeals which it emits every minute and which is distracting even through three closed doors (it is in constant use often up to 2300 hours)".*

7 August 1978	*"Ref 29th June 1978 entry, whatever was 'done' didn't do the job! For the infernal machine continues to sing its irritating song. May I request another try or perhaps to further consider the machine being replaced".*
7 August 1978	*"On 10th Nov 78 a presentation by UK MAMs Officers RAF Lyneham is to be given to members of Derbyshire & Nottinghamshire RAFA and invited guests. Part of the evenings activities will be a demonstration of Polish dancing and singing. May the Mess piano now housed in No.2 garage be renovated and made presentable for the occasion?"*
22 February 1979	*"a) The BBC1 Television has distorted sound and needs adjustment or replacement, b) The lighting is made more pleasant in the BBC2 and ITV rooms by the addition of a standard lamp in each room".*

The Eighties

7 March 1980	*"I should like to raise again the question of purchasing a piano for the Mess. Whatever contrary opinions may have been explained in the past, I believe that there is a need for a piano, both for member's personal use and enjoyment and also for use at Mess functions. It is not satisfactory that when a musical function takes place, the PMC has to seek permission to borrow an old piano from the Community Centre".*
20 June 1983	*"May I suggest that now it is midsummer-eve, the inmates are allowed to wear 'Planters Rig' in the evening".*
5 April 1984	*"May I suggest that we do not, if I suspect that we are – murder those beautiful trees just to extend the Mess for our pleasure for the Summer Ball".*

The PMC's reply was:

6 April 1984	*"Too late! The evil deed is done. Whilst I share your views, this decision was not taken lightly. There will be other occasions such as the Annual Reception and Conferences when the re-landscaping will be to our benefit".*
18 June 1984	*"May I suggest that 'Planters Rig' is instituted ASAP".*

The final entry in the suggestions book was a reply from the PMC:

11 May 1984	*"To be considered at the Committee meeting 16th May 84".*

The Airmen's Mess was situated at the end of the parade square near the main gate, with the dining hall on the right and the NAAFI club on the left, later christened the 'Fosse Club' it was extensively extended in 1962 during the stations major rebuilding programme. Facilities included a licensed bar, snack bar and space for discos and live acts. A Corporals Club was also incorporated into the building. A 'Cold War' underground 'Passive' food store was also constructed with the access hatch sited outside the right hand entrance. It is reputed to extend out under the parade square and there are unconfirmed reports of a tunnel linking it with the Station Headquarters. Several former Airmen still have tins of food 'raided' from this supply and when the time came for it to be inspected for an

TO THE MESS

Christmas
Menu 1972

Royal Air Force Newton

inventory, there was hardly anything left! At Christmas the mess held an annual military tradition of the Officers being 'invited' in to the mess hall to act as waiters serving the airmen with food and drinks, an event where you could have your jar of Watney's Ale refilled by non other than the Station Commander.

At the opposite end of the square, the Sergeant's Mess was relocated from building 59 into a brand new complex nearby, built in the stark post war style. The Rt Hon Sir Hugh Fraser officially opened the building in April 1964. Apart from the formal dining in nights and dances, the three messes also played host to more light-hearted functions. In 1995 when the Officer's and Airmen's Mess' closed down, the Sergeants Mess remained open to become the station's new 'Combined Mess'. Limited sleeping, catering and bar facilities as well as the occasional function kept the building in use until the resident units departed in 2000.

"The farewell party nights were often unihibited affairs and I found it imprudent for the CO to appear in the Mess just then"

Construction work to extend the
Fosse Club at the Airmen's Mess,
25th September 1962.

Construction of the new Sergeant's Mess, 1964.

The Airmen's Mess

Terry Johnson, who now lives in Western Australia served at Newton in the early 1960s in the Training Aids Workshop; part of the electrical/mechanical support for the Guided Weapons School. He recalls "I used to enjoy walking down to Bingham for a beer, and I won £5 for naming the other-ranks mess as 'The Fosse Club'. Our resident metalsmith, Chief Technician, Peter Restorick made a copper plate depicting a Roman eagle to mark the entrance – I wonder if it is still there? He also made a brass desk ornament for the CO which consisted of a V-Bomber balanced on a narrow spike with its bomb doors open, from which came a thin rod and attached to the end was a missile, a fantastic piece of workmanship!"

Above: **The entrance to the dining hall, 2008.** Adam Davey

Opposite page:

Top left: **Malaysian students enjoying the Christmas party, 1972.** Author's collection

Above left: **The Christmas party, 1972.** Author's collection

Left **Seating in the first floor cinema.** T O'Brien

Bottom: **Exterior view from September 1962 showing construction work in progress to extend the Fosse Club.** Author's collection

Top right: **One of the round windows in the first floor washrooms.** T O'Brien

Right: **Staircase detail.** T O'Brien

The Sergeant's Mess

The Sergeant's Mess has had two homes on the base. The first one was in Building 59, an original 1930s structure built with two accommodation annexes either side of the main building. It remained in use until it moved into a new building, opened on 21st April 1964 by the Rt Hon Sir Hugh Fraser. Building 59 was then converted into the station community centre.

Top left: **The new Sergeant's Mess in 2002 before the vandals and graffiti artists arrived!** T O'Brien

Lower left: **The newly completed Mess in April 1964.** Author's collection

Top right: **Window detail above the main entrance to Building 59.** T O'Brien

Lower right: **More window detail from the side of Building 59.** T O'Brien

Below: **Building 59 as seen in 2008.** T O'Brien

The Officer's Mess

Above: **AVM Atcherley and AM Sir Dermot Boyle, Chief of the Air Staff at the 1958 Annual Dinner of Nottingham University Air Squadron.** Newton archives

Left: **An invitation to the 1958 NUAS annual dinner.** EMUAS collection

Opposite page:

Top: **Exterior view, 2002.** T O'Brien

Upper left: **The main entrance, 2002.** T O'Brien

Bottom left: **The east wing still showing signs of wartime camouflage in 2002.** T O'Brien

Upper right: **Window detail on the West Wing; 2009.** T O'Brien

Lower right: **The window above the main entrance.** T O'Brien

Bottom right: **Sign for the officer's mess car park which was constructed on the site of the wartime standby house.** T O'Brien

NOTTINGHAM UNIVERSITY
AIR SQUADRON

ANNUAL DINNER
1958

OFFICERS MESS
CAR PARK
100 METRES
ON LEFT

Building 27

An aerial view from August 2008.
T O'Brien

Sign Here!

Graham Norbury of Bunny once 'served' at Royal Air Force Newton for a short period in early 1973, but not with the RAF. Graham takes up the story:

"At the time, I was a young Executive Officer in the Ministry of Agriculture Fisheries and Food at Chalfont Drive, Nottingham when there was an outbreak of Swine Vasicular Disease SVD. SVD only infects pigs, but the way of dealing with it was similar to Foot and Mouth. There were a number of cases to the East of Nottingham and Chalfont Drive was deemed not suitable as a Disease Centre."

"Apart from its location, the choice of RAF Newton was a bit of a surprise as it was still operational. We were located in 'Building 27', the old wartime Armoury which was reputed to be haunted! Most of the building was used as storage, but we occupied the top floor where we could observe some of the flying activities, although partially obscured by the hangars, not that we had much time to watch. I recall that one part of the lower storey looked a bit like the sort of Ops Rooms you see in films with a gallery from which the Controllers operated and senior officers observed."

"We had arrived with a limited amount of furniture and supplies (no computers in those days) and the RAF supplied extra furniture and the all important electric kettle – all signed for in triplicate! Our job was to support the Vets and help trace stock which may have come into contact with pigs with SVD, order supplies of coal and railway sleepers (to burn the slaughtered pigs) and the obnoxious disinfectant Lysol used to clean premises. We were fully operational by the time the Vets arrived later that morning."

"On arrival, the ministry admin staff had been made honorary members of the Sergeant's Mess with magnificent lunches at around 35p and the CO offered the ministry vets the same deal. On querying why they could not use the Officer's Mess instead, they were told in no uncertain terms that the food in the Sergeant's Mess was far better and cheaper and in fact even better in the Airmen's Mess!"

"I think that we were there for about two weeks, before being sent off to Chesterfield to set up another centre. However, we were not done with RAF Newton, as a few weeks later I got a call from the base wanting to know whether we had one of their tables. My response was that we had loads of tables which were standard issue for both the Civil Service and the Forces so how would I identify it? "No problem", the voice at the other end replied, "Its reference number is…" This turned out to be a combination of about 15 letters and figures and sure enough there it was enjoying a holiday in our own stores!"

"the RAF supplied extra furniture and the all important electric kettle – all signed for in triplicate!"

The Station Farm

Long before 'Organic Farm shops' became fashionable, RAF Newton was one of the few stations that had its own farm, which not only provided the station with fresh produce, but other local RAF airfields too, such as RAF Syerston.

Opposite: **Lawson's Barn Farm that has stood empty since the Woolley family departed for Scotland in the mid 1980s. The family ran the station farm from here for many years.** T O'Brien

Below: **The first Barley crop for the Station Farm being harvested in what is known locally as 'Hangar Field' by a Massey Ferguson 780 in 1964. The 'White House' in Newton village and AMQs on Fairway Crescent can be seen in the distance.** Author's collection

Bottom: **Building 39, which was used by the Woolley family as the Station Farm shop in the 1960s to sell fresh produce such as strawberries. Jan Krupa and other Polish airmen believe the original wartime use for this building was as an overflow gaol for the main guard house or for gas defence training. In the 1980s and 90s it was used by the photographic club and 1936 Sqn ATC as a radio hut. The field behind it was farmed for a long time and was home to the station pig farm in the late 1950s, being run by Dennis Dawson.** T O'Brien

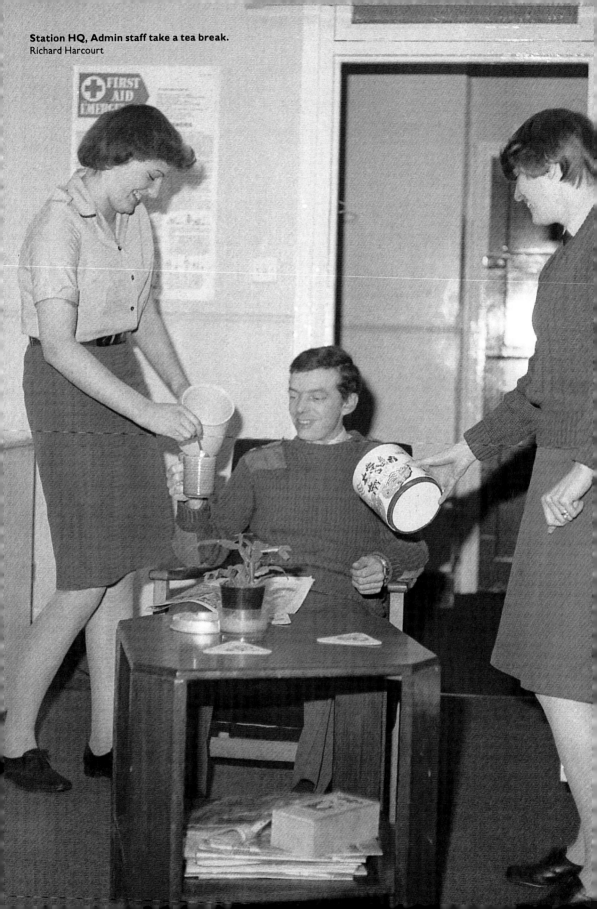

Station HQ, Admin staff take a tea break.
Richard Harcourt

Have a Break...

Heads look up to see gold and silver bursting out of the stars before a shower of red, white and blue sparkles across the autumn sky in a thunderous show. Flames dance into the cold night air as several planks of wood collapse into the bonfire amidst red sparks adding excitement amongst the crowd. Today as I stand upon the grass behind the old School of Education block and Fairway Crescent, memories flood back of watching the annual bonfire night that was staged here for station personnel and families. An event you always anticipated as you watched the pile of wood grow over the preceding weeks.

Over sixty years the station always provided an alternative range of recreational activities for those who wanted to make their own entertainment on site ranging from the mess to an activity club. Situated between a barrack block and the Airmen's Mess, Newton had its own 'Astra' cinema that overlooked the parade square featuring the word 'CINEMA' in large raised letters above the entrance. Local resident Dave Mumford remembers it well; "*As my father (ex-army) worked at Newton as a civilian gardener for the CO, I was eligible to attend Newton's Children Christmas party. All the children were picked up by an RAF coach from the White Lion pub in Bingham and dropped off at the cinema where we watched films and were given presents*". The building was also used occasionally as an amateur theatre before being pulled down circa 1964 and transferred to the upper storey of the Airmen's Mess.

The block that used to house the Sergeant's Mess until 1964 was converted into a Community Centre and Kindergarten and Church of England Chapel, which helped to add to the inclusive atmosphere of community spirit on the camp. The centre hosted a variety of activities that included a Thrift Shop, Coffee Shop, the local Air Scout troop, Mother and Toddler groups, Crèche and Playgroup. The wives of station personnel had their own club called the 'Wives' Club'. They met on alternate Monday evenings in the Community Centre where they enjoyed various activities and entertainments. On Tuesday afternoons all ladies were welcome to take part in Ladies' Badminton in the Sports Centre and take part in swimming sessions on Wednesday afternoons at Bingham Leisure Centre. Baby Clinics along with Ante-Natal and Family Planning Clinics were also provided in the Station Medical Centre.

Members of the Wives' Club also organised a Cheshire Homes roster every Wednesday afternoon to make tea and coffee for the residents of the local Cheshire Home at Holme Lodge on Adbolton Lane, West Bridgford. Over many years Newton built up close links with the home and organised many functions with them. One fine summer afternoon in July 1988, residents were invited to a tea party in the station commander's garden where they enjoyed the opportunity for a good chat and to meet some new faces.

For the more practical individuals the Handicrafts club not only gave the opportunity to construct a variety of objects, but also the chance to help the local community. They would construct projects in the old 'Link' Trainer building. Each Christmas cricket bats, slides, swings, table tennis equipment, dolls houses and go-karts were constructed, and then presented to local children's homes at Brick House, Radcliffe-on-Trent and Broughton House in Newark. Personnel from the station also made the kind gesture of giving away bags of kindling wood to local pensioners. Other activity clubs included the Newton Art Club who regularly exhibited their paintings and drawings at various open days.

Aircraft model-making has also been a popular pastime whether they are plastic Airfix kits or the balsa wood Keil-Kraft examples. In 1952, Newton hosted the national Model Championships, which allowed competing entrants the chance to fly their large radio controlled aircraft from the grass runways. For many years the station model club used the small building that stands on the corner of the road junction next to the new Sergeants Mess. Prior to the club using this building, it had been used as a 'Farm Shop' by the tenant farmer to sell produce from the Station's Farm. The field opposite this building was farmed for crops but around 1960 was used as the station pig farm. With the first wheat crop in 1964, the station was one of the few in the RAF to have its very own farm enabling it to supply itself with fresh produce. Along with the model club, the Photography Club also used the building as a base before the air cadets moved in to house their radio facilities.

For mechanically minded personnel, the Motor Club provided an opportunity to practice vehicle maintenance. Housed in the MT sheds, the club would often take on projects for other units which helped both parties financially and for the instructional value. During their 'day job' the MT section often received awards for their work such as the MT Efficiency Award, presented by the AOC No.24 Group on 12th June 1970. Newton also hosted a Motorcycle Club, which met in hangar 3 at 1800 hours on the first Tuesday in the month and often visited local bike events at Donington Park and beyond.

Musical tastes were also catered for with Station's official band in the 1960s comprising of regular servicemen who played at many official functions on and off the station. But this activity was not exclusive to the adults as around two dozen youngsters aged 6 to 15 formed the RAF Newton Junior Band in 1966, the only such band in the RAF at the time. Trained by Mr English, a civilian bandmaster with the RAF Musical Services, the band gained a reputation to be proud of. Every year they would be invited to play at garden fetes, schools, hospitals, nursing homes and ATC parades. Other pastimes to keep the servicemen's children occupied included the 'Newton Youth Club'. Who also participated in station fetes by organising fun activities to raise money for the RAF Benevolent Fund such as the 'Chicken Run' where its members dressed up as chickens and suffered the 'agony' of being hit by wet sponges thrown by onlookers.

On the domestic front the station Post office was opened 27th May 1957 with Mrs L Hodd as the postmistress. Then on 6th April 1966, the Lady Mayoress of Nottingham, Mrs W Derbyshire opened the station's new NAAFI Supermarket. Located near the main gate, the store sold a range of food and dry goods. It remained open for business serving the base until it closed in 1995, then after lying disused for five years it was extensively refurbished for 1936 Squadron as their new home.

In the days before cash points, the station had its own branch of the National Westminster Bank on site. Sited in an old wartime wooden building near the water tower, this branch provided a much needed convenience if you didn't have time to drive to the main NatWest branch in Bingham or Radcliffe. Or if you just wanted a good read, then you could borrow a book from the Station Library that was open five days a week in the Station Education Centre. The summer of 1988 saw the Station publish the first copy of its own glossy magazine called the *Newton Courier*, which replaced earlier more basic newsletters to keep everyone up to date with Station news.

And there were plenty of sports activities to participate in at the excellent sports centre. Situated in a hangar, most kinds of sport took place from weight-lifting, football, basketball, to squash, tennis and badminton. Most of these sports also had a specialist club that you could attend in your leisure time such Aerobics or the Shotokan Karate Club and the Tae Kwon-do Club. These sports facilities were not exclusive to station personnel though. For in 1972, Manager Dave MacKay brought the Nottingham Forest football team here once a week to use the excellent sports centre and keep his team in shape with a two-hour test of strength and stamina. I remember many a Friday night in the centre, when the air cadets regularly used the sports facilities for football or badminton matches as well as training for the Duke of Edinburgh award scheme. The station's original gymnasium was housed in a building next to the emergency exit onto the A46 on the officer's married quarter's estate. This building was later converted to house an indoor rifle range, which was still in use by the Air Training Corps as late as 1983.

Outdoor tennis courts were constructed during the war next to the officer's mess plus some more near to the old Sgt's Mess. They were originally started by Italian prisoners of war and finished off by German POWs from a camp at nearby Saxondale. Aleksander Gertner remembers using these courts during the war as he often played tennis with some WRENs, who were the daughters of the Chief Medical Officer at Saxondale Hospital. A squash court was also housed near to the Officers Mess in a converted wartime building and in front of this was the football pitch. Football was another popular distraction from the hectic training schedule for the Polish airmen during the war. One Pole who enjoyed these breaks on the playing field was Mietek Pawlow who went on to play for Notts County after the war. While the cricket ground and pavilion was sited on the opposite side of the road behind the barrack blocks. Station personnel would often use these facilities in the evenings or on the armed forces traditional Wednesday afternoon sports session. An annual sports day was also held giving everyone a chance to compete together. Teams representing individual sports often took part in other service and civilian championships. One Station event was the inaugural RAF Newton WRAF Challenge Trophy was held on April 14th 1988 where 18 WRAF and 15 RAF personnel took part in a rugby match.

In the same year the Combined Services Chess Championships returned to Newton for the first time since 1969 and were held in the Community Centre from 7th to 12th April. Thirty-four competitors entered the championships, of which four were Army and the other thirty were RAF including one WRAF. The reigning champion Corporal John Treasurer an RAF Policeman from Kinloss and was eventually beaten by Cpl Alec Toll of Brize Norton. Having its own golf course situated on the strip of land between the Sergeant's Mess and the Officer's Mess, also provided many with another sporting opportunity and in 1972 the station golf team won the East Midlands Golf League trophy.

The station also hosted the RAF's National Angling Championships in the same year with nearly 600 anglers pegged on both banks of the River Trent between Burton Joyce and Gunthorpe Bridge, which was opened by Edward Prince of Wales in 1927. Here the river is alive with boats and visitors to the Unicorn Hotel and Anchor public houses. Newton's Canoe Club also used this part of the river when they weren't using Bingham Leisure Centre. While the Dinghy Sailing Club had an Enterprise Dinghy moored at Newark Marina. The Station was also affiliated to three rowing clubs including the Nottingham Boat Club, with several personnel entering for the annual RAF Rowing Championships.

From time to time the station would also arrange excursions off camp for the more adventurous, such as the 1965 expedition to climb 'Ben Nevis' in Scotland. In the late 1980s the Mountaineering Club travelled to the Austrian Alps before returning via the Rhine, Belgium and Holland. The Diving Club also travelled abroad to seek more exotic facilities than those at the local baths, when they visited Gibraltar in 1988.

In the early seventies, the 'Tug of War' team often challenged local teams at village fetes around the county. One mile away at Saxondale Hospital in 1972, they were beaten yet again at the hospitals open day by their old rivals the 'Black Diamonds' of East Bridgford, who had not been beaten by anyone in 8 years. However at the Car Colston and Screveton Village Festival, Newton retaliated by beating them for the first time during a 'nail-biting' contest. Following up this success in October 1972, they emerged as the RAF Training Command's champions of the year.

Christmas time saw the station round off its year of social events by looking after its children with a 'Children's Christmas Party', where clowns and circus horses delighted all. The 1966 party was organised by a team led by Sqn Ldr D R McCall, OC Basic Studies Squadron and held on 17th December for 386 children of the station and 20 children nominated by local RAFA branches. Another tradition was for the children from Newton Playgroup to perform a Nativity play at the Senior Citizens Christmas party. As I turn round and head back past the airmen's married quarters I wonder if the new civilian community has the same range of activities to hand. Whatever the current situation is, years ago the RAF base had an enviable self-sufficiency in its activities which in turn strengthened the community spirit.

Above: **The RAF Model aircraft championships, 1952.** Author's collection

Right: **Administrative staff from Station HQ enjoy a musical night out in a local Bingham public house.** J Francis collection

Bottom right: **Newton's Junior band visit the Cheshire Home at west Bridgford to entertain the residents, 1967.** Author's collection

Opposite page:

Top left: **RAF Newton's expedition to Ben Nevis, 1965.** Author's collection

Top right: **Newton's Youth Club organise a 'Chicken Run' at the Station Fete, 2nd August 1967.** Author's collection

Lower left: **On 19th December 1969, the Handicrafts club present some toys they made to the Children's Home at Broughton House, Newark.** Author's collection

Bottom: **The station band, 1965.** Author's collection

Opposite page:

Top: **The sports arena signage on No.5 Hangar.**
T O'Brien

Bottom: **The cricket field, now under the plough
and the pavilion constructed circa 1982.**
T O'Brien

This page:

Left: **The station Sports day, Wednesday 27th July
1966.** Author's collection

Below: **The squash courts opposite the Officers
Mess, 2002.** T O'Brien

Left: **The Massed Pipes and Drums of the RAF, which consisted of 5 or 6 bands – a scene never to be witnessed again! The bands all met up at Newton, stayed and practiced there prior to HM the Queen's Silver Jubilee Review of the Royal Air Force at RAF Finningley on 29th July 1977. What a sight and sound!** Richard Harcourt

Bottom left: **The Children's Christmas party, 17th December 1966.** Author's collection

Below: **Jim Pickering and his Wallis autogyro G-ATTB at the 1968 open day.** Newton archives

Bottom: **The rear of the Community Centre that looks out on to the parade square, the scene of many a disco!** T O'Brien

DETACHMENT HEADQUARTERS

The front door. J Proudlock

Key Personnel

The first Station Commander at Newton was Group Captain G T Tyrrell, a veteran of the First World War and was officially appointed in December 1940 despite having been at the station for several months. When the Polish Air Force arrived in July 1941, Newton had in effect two station commanders, RAF Group Captain, E B Grenfell and a Polish Group Captain, S Cwynar who was in charge of the large Polish presence. After the war as the numbers of personnel drastically reduced on the station, the ranks of the station commanders also reflected this, by having lower ranking officers such as Squadron Leaders and Wing Commanders in charge. It was only when the technical training school arrived in 1960, thus increasing the size of the base that the rank of Group Captain returned.

As the new Station Commander moving into 19 Newton Gardens in 1989, Group Captain John Martin AFC, Bsc wrote a foreword in the *Newton Courier*, the Station magazine, which included the following extract, "*It is a pleasure and a privilege to take command of RAF Newton. In the past, like many in the 'Lincolnshire Air Force', I have driven past RAF Newton many times and wondered what went on here. It has been a revelation these last few weeks to learn about the many and varied tasks which the Station and its parented units (Syerston) carry out. In particular, I have been tremendously impressed by the 'can-do' attitude, high standards and community spirit, from this sense of commitment and involvement*". John, a former Vulcan pilot concluded his foreword by wishing everyone at Newton a successful and enjoyable tour at RAF Newton.

Gp Capt Martin's successor in March 1991 was Gp Capt Philip Langrill OBE. Today at his home in Anglesey, he looks back at his time at Newton and thinks about his overwhelming memory of the station. "*After a few years in the service, you can quickly recognise the tenor of an RAF Station. Various factors contribute to a visitor's initial impression, including the manner in which you are received at the guardroom, the general appearance of the place and the demeanour of the personnel. Newton starred in all those respects. I had visited RAF Newton only once before taking command. That first visit was made during the distant days of 1962 when I was a young flying instructor at RAF Valley flying the de Havilland Vampire. One of my flying students was getting married in Nottingham and I had agreed to be his Best Man. As it seemed to make sense to spend the pre-nuptial night at Newton's Officers' Mess I set off on the long cross country drive from Anglesey to Nottinghamshire as soon as flying ceased at Valley. Some miles from Newton I ran into dense fog and crawled along painfully from cats-eye to cats-eye. Eventually I was flagged down by a dripping figure by the roadside. It turned out to be the bridegroom of the morrow! His car had broken down and by a fluke I found him stranded by the roadside. I ended up driving him to his wedding and lending him my car for use during his honeymoon. Sadly, a flying accident in Hong Kong eventually claimed his life.*"

"*When, towards the end of my RAF career I was promoted to the rank of Group Captain I was delighted to be told that I could probably expect to be appointed to command a flying station and was given a hint about which airfield it might be. I waited with happy anticipation for the posting to be confirmed and was surprised when the news came that rather than returning to flying I was to fill the appointment of Air Advisor to the British High Commissioner in India. The incumbent had resigned and there was an urgent need to fill the post quickly. While the diplomatic appointment in India provided much fascination and unique opportunities to travel throughout south Asia, I was not prepared to let the chance of a flying command slip through my fingers. Eventually the Air Secretary's department informed me that after my sojourn in India I should command RAF Newton. I was ecstatic."*

"From the very start, Newton seemed to be a delightful place. Gp Capt John Martin gave me a warm welcome and during the week we over-lapped at Newton, I had ample opportunity to explore the estate and meet everyone. It was an attractive station of manicured lawns, mature trees and well-tended flower beds. Although possessing a relatively small acreage, it was a busy place with a large variety of courses running at any given time in the major schools. The diversity and quality of course content was impressive. Above all, it was clearly a very happy station". After the traditional ceremony of taking down the outgoing CO's pennant and raising that of the new Station Commander, the two Group Captains went to the main door of Station Headquarters and ceremoniously handed over the large silver key which symbolised access to the seat of command. *"I am not aware of such a 'key ceremony' at other RAF stations",* recalls Gp Capt Langrill. *"The élan and dedication of the staff was clearly evident throughout the station. The basic training of RAF Police School recruits gave the place an overtly military feel, not least because squads of 'under training' basic policemen were forever marching or jogging in squads around the station's roads. Newton was probably the smallest station on which I have served, but it was often densely populated and every major building was in use. The population varied according to the training course loading. That said, it was often intriguing to speculate on just where all the personnel actually were: the station's roads were frequently deserted and it was not until cease work that personnel would flood out of the various schools and offices!"*

During this period the station was facing an uncertain future, as it was one of several locations on a training base closure list. Would it be Halton, Scampton or Newton, who were going to be the winners and losers? Had the end come at last? All because the Government had announced their 'Options for Change' policy in July 1990, which planned to reduce the size of the UK Armed Forces following the collapse of communism with the Berlin Wall. It was the plans intention to shrink RAF numbers from 89,000 to 75,000 in two years, then as the Cold War continued to thaw a major rationalisation and relocation programme of the RAF's training establishments was proposed in a series of Government Defence Reviews. Gp Capt Langrill remembers this, *"Before taking command of RAF Newton I was, of course briefed by personnel at Command Headquarters. The Command staff officers informed me that as RAF Newton had a guaranteed future I was to be awarded an enhanced 'estates' budget to permit the condition of all the station's buildings to be brought up to scratch. This included the expensive re-roofing of all five hangars. During the first annual inspection of the station, which happened shortly after my assumption of command, I was advised that the progress made in refurbishing the camp would be the focus of the next annual inspection. By then considerable funds* had been spent on the necessary works services and contracts were let for work yet to be started. I seem to remember that three of our five hangars had been re-roofed by the time the closure of the station became common knowledge. I was of course mortified by the news that our compact, efficient, mature, happy station was to be abandoned and I did all I could to make the many merits of the place clear to those in authority over me. It was all to no avail."

Finally he recalls the time he had to retire and bid the station farewell. *"The EMUAS personnel built a replica aeroplane on wheels, sufficiently big and mobile for me to be pulled around the station in it, waving to the personnel who came out of the various schools and sections to see me off. An inescapable part of handing over command was to check the petty cash. So, my successor Gp Capt 'Sid' Adcock and I solemnly went to the accounts section and reconciled the holding of petty cash (loose change, it seemed to me!), including the postage stamps and then I was able to sign over command of the station. It seemed odd to me that we did not count the aircraft, hangars or search dogs, merely the petty cash! There followed a touching ceremony at which a piper played a lament while my pennant was lowered from the flag-staff to be replaced by that of my successor. Then my wife and I climbed aboard my private car and we set off for Anglesey and retirement. All that had filled my life for so many years had dwindled down quite abruptly to the moment of farewell and departure. Despite the exciting and colourful appointments I had previously held, my command of Newton was quite easily the most memorable period of my thirty-five year RAF career. The RAF working Dog Championships always seemed to be held on sunlit days when the manicured lawns and brilliant flower beds were seen at their best. Training targets were consistently met, discipline was excellent and moral was high. But above all, it was the élan, dedication and support of the station personnel that I remember with most gratitude and affection. It is often said that a Commanding Officer has an exceedingly lonely job. I did not find it so at RAF Newton."*

When Group Captain C B 'Sid' Adcock aged 51 took over command of the base on 2nd April 1993 from Gp Capt Philip Langrill, the station numbers had already fallen to just 550 service personnel and 150 civilians compared with 1200 service personnel and 180 civilian staff in 1967. Gp Capt Adcock takes up the story, *"When I assumed command of the station it had already been announced that, as a result of a study into 'Ground Training in the RAF', Newton was to be run down with a view to eventual closure, along with several ground training stations in the RAF. At Newton, however, there was a complication, in that the unit was home to East Midlands University Air Squadron (EMUAS) and No.7 Air Experience Flight (7 AEF), and there were no other suitable airfields in the catchment area to which these units could be transferred. As an interim measure, therefore it was decided to retain the airfield and hangars within a small enclave that would be retained by the RAF while the rest of the site was decommissioned."*

"Much of my time as Station Commander was spent not in running the station – OC Admin Wing and his staff care of much of the day-to-day management – but in liaising with the local community. As the only remaining RAF Station in Nottinghamshire, Newton enjoyed a very high standing in the county, and I was consequently deluged with invitations to various civic events. In my two years in command, I attended more

Above: **RAF Balfour Beatty! The A46 dualling contractors occupy the Station Headquarters; using it as their operations hub; July 2009.** T O'Brien

Below: **Station Headquarters as seen in 1999 when it had been re-named Detachment Headquarters.** J Proudlock

civic functions than I had in my entire life up to that point. Lunches, dinners, balls, parades, memorial and commemorative services, beatings of the retreat, sporting and social events – you name it, I attended! To repay some of this hospitality, we held every year a Station Civic Dignitaries Day, to which we invited all the mayors in the local area."

"For me as the Station Commander, the fact that Newton and Syerston were flying units was a great attraction. Before taking up the appointment I had carried out a short flying refresher course with the Central Flying School at RAF Scampton, so when I arrived at Newton I was already qualified to fly the Bulldog with EMUAS. In due course I added the Chipmunks of 7 AEF to my list of qualifications, followed by the Robin, used for aero-towing at Syerston. I also qualified to fly the two gliders used at Syerston, the Vigilant and the Viking. Furthermore, as the Station Commander, I automatically became the Chairman of the Four Counties Gliding Club, so I also learned to fly some of their gliders as well. Being able to fly several times a week not only relieved some of the more tedious administrative aspects of the Station Commander's lot but also allowed me to reciprocate some of the hospitality I received locally by flying the occasional civic dignitary in a Bulldog."

"One of the main difficulties I faced during my tour of duty as Station Commander was the question of how to maintain morale on the unit when it was faced with so much uncertainty. With the support of my staff, a series of high profile events were instituted that would provide a focus of activity for the people of the station and help them maintain a pride in their unit. These included the final and highly successful Air Day that was appreciated by the whole community. We were lucky to enjoy perfect weather for the event, which drew several thousand spectators from all over the East Midlands. Throughout all this period of frenetic activity I was well supported by my wife and family. At the time, both my sons were serving in the military; the eldest James, as an Engineering Officer in the RAF, and the youngest, Brian, as Junior Officer in the Royal Marines. Both sons were able to attend the Officers Mess Summer Ball of 1993, making it not only a very enjoyable family reunion but also the setting for an unusual and attractive photograph for the family album."

"After much prevarication, it was eventually decided by HQ PTC that with effect from 1st April 1995, RAF Cranwell would parent the Newton enclave, thus bringing to an end my time in command. So, before any of the major units at Newton left the Station for their new locations, we held a farewell dinner in the Officer's Mess that was attended by the Air Officer Training, Air Vice Marshal John May, several former Station Commanders, and a number of dignatries from the local area who had a particular affinity with the Station. Before going into dinner, we took part in a sunset ceremony in front of the Mess that involved a symbolic lowering of the ensign for the last time. For me, it was a particularly poignant moment, bringing to an end two of the most demanding but enjoyable years of my life, and leaving me with an experience that I shall never forget."

A series of three detachment commanders then took over, before the base finally closed whilst under the command of Squadron Leader Colin Rawe.

RAF NEWTON

STATION COMMANDERS

Group Captain G T Tyrrell	12th December 1940
Group Captain E B Grenfell	21st July 1941
Group Captain C E Barraclough	1st September 1944
Squadron Leader J F Honchin	19th December 1946
Wing Commander E W Wootton DFC	13th February 1947
Wing Commander W M Collins DFC	20th August 1947
Wing Commander E F E Barnard	3rd December 1948
Wing Commander N C Harding	20th February 1951
Wing Commander R C F Lister DFC	6th September 1953
Squadron Leader R M Pugh	29th October 1954
Wing Commander T M Buchanan	20th December 1954
Wing Commander R J E Boulding	19th December 1956
Squadron Leader A Philips	24th October 1958
Wing Commander N F Searle	25th April 1960
Group Captain R G K Smith	24th May 1961
Group Captain R F J Barber OBE	7th January 1963
Group Captain E H Jenkins	29th November 1965
Group Captain A Fry OBE	21st June 1968
Group Captain W K MacTaggart MBE	12th February 1971
Group Captain T D Ward	19th February 1973
Group Captain L A Ferguson OBE	4th July 1975
Group Captain R G Bowyer AMBIM	5th May 1978
Group Captain J Delafield MRAeS	9th May 1980
Group Captain S W T Holding BSc	7th May 1982
Group Captain D H Wardill Ceng MIEE MIMechE	23rd November 1984
Group Captain R E Holliday OBE	7th August 1987
Group Captain J F S Martin AFC BSc	3rd February 1989
Group Captain P Langrill OBE	22nd March 1991
Group Captain C B Adcock BA FIMGT	2nd April 1993

DETACHMENT COMMANDERS

Squadron Leader R D Gammage BSc	2nd August 1995
Squadron Leader A Clarke	1st April 1996
Squadron Leader C J Rawe	5th October 1998

Group Captain Wardill departs as Group Captain Holliday arrives. Newton Archives

This page, clockwise from top right:

Group Captain MacTaggart supplies more Watney's Ale at the 1972 Christmas party in the Airmen's Mess. Author's collection

Group Captains Barber and Jenkins, 29th November 1965. Author's collection

The rear of the Station Commanders residence at 19 Newton Gardens, 2002. T O'Brien

Group Captain John Martin's card. Author's collection

Opposite page, from top:

Group Captain Tyrrell, the first station commander and his admin staff, 1940. Author's collection

Wing Commander Barnard accompanies the Secretary of State for Air, Arthur Henderson at the 1949 'At Home' day. Author's collection

Group Captain J F S Martin
AFC BSC RAF

STATION COMMANDER   0949 20771
RAF NEWTON   EXT 201

This page:

Right: **The old red GPO telephone boxes by the Airmen's Mess.**
Artist – T O'Brien GAvA

Below: **A side view of the station headquarters in 2008.** Adam Davey

Opposite page:

Top left: **The station headquarters personnel circa 1963 with SAC John Francis, top right.**
J Francis collection

Top right: **Operators in the telephone exchange, late 1970s.**
Richard Harcourt

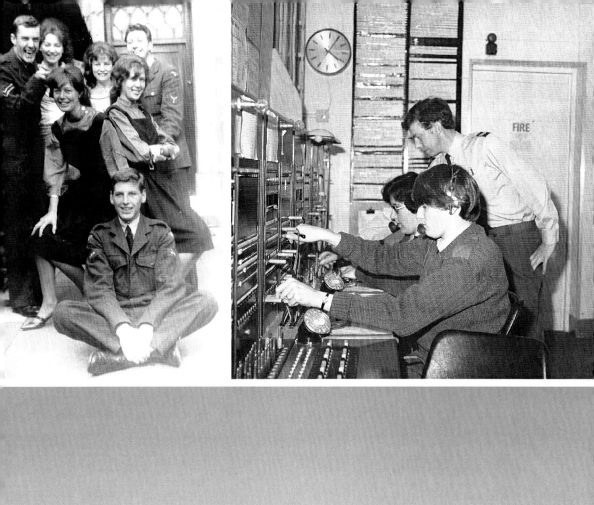

The Officers Married Quarters in August 2008. T O'Brien

Country Living

What was it like living in the Married Quarters of a Royal Air Force Station sited in the countryside? Here are two observations from an Officer and Non-Commissioned Officer (NCO) who lived in contrasting types of house.

Group Captain Phil Langrill, Station Commander from March 1991 to April 1993 lived in the largest of the older 1930s Officers Married Quarters (OMQs) at 19 Newton Gardens Officers. Gp Capt Langrill recalls what it was like living in the Station Commander's house. *"My OMQ at 19 Newton Gardens was a three-storey masterpiece which, I was told had been based on plans drawn up by Sir Edwin Lutyens who, having designed the Imperial city of New Delhi to be the centrepiece of the British Empire, presided over the committee which designed the standard RAF Station of the pre-war era. I believe that his designs of houses, messes and so forth have never been bettered. The Station Commander's residence was spacious and elegant. I do not know what differentiates a lounge from a drawing room, but we most certainly had a drawing room than a lounge! In the dining room we could seat over sixteen in comfort. So, in summary, the house had an ample kitchen, a spacious drawing room, a more than adequate dining room, a useful study, a noble staircase and a downstairs toilet. The second floor had three sizeable bedrooms and two bathrooms. The top (third) storey had four bedrooms but was neither heated nor equipped with toilet facilities. It was a privilege to have lived in such an imposing house, which fitted so well the needs of a Commanding Officer."*

"For day-to-day use, when only Joan and I occupied the place, we tended to relax in the study, which was of a less extravagant size than the public rooms and much easier to keep warm. The house was still fitted with sash windows of pre-War style. These permitted the free flow of air through the overlapping windows so our efforts to keep the temperature inside the house above arctic levels caused the ancient central heating system to consume an enormous amount of oil! But when official visitors descended on us, or on the occasions when we entertained station personnel and local luminaries the house came into its own. We would prepare a roaring fire in the lounge, fuelled with logs brought in from Newton and Syerston airfields by the groundsmen. Also, when our two sons descended on us with their undergraduate colleagues every room was filled!"

"We played host to a variety of senior officials, including the Roman Catholic Bishop to the three Armed Services. The dinner guests on that occasion included members of Newton's RC congregation and a Catholic Canon who was attached in some way to Southwell Minster. I pondered anxiously how to address the great man and consulting informed opinion on the subject, was assured that I should call him 'Your Beatitude'. Yet, when I met him on the windswept platform of Newark railway station, he shook my hand vigorously and announced that I should call him "Frank!" He was an easy guest to have on board. As we only used a small proportion of our 'batting' allowance in the house (i.e. we did not draw all the staffing support we were entitled to from the Officers' Mess) we were able to use a Mess chef and steward for official entertainment. The chefs relished the opportunity to show off their skills catering for the Officers' Mess. On several occasions, guests left our house remarking that they had never been given a better meal!"

"After a few months in the post, I decided to revive the old practise of 'calling'. This had pertained throughout the British Empire and in RAF terms, required officers to 'call' on their CO both when they arrived on strength and when they were leaving their appointment. Their wives would similarly 'call' on the CO's wife. This procedure, although thought by many to be stuffy and outdated, had the advantage of permitting the CO to meet newly appointed officers and to say goodbye to those leaving his command. My 'revival' took the form of welcome-in cocktail parties which, although went very well, were easier to start than to stop! It proved necessary to stick strictly to the start and finish times and to turn off the supply of the 'stuff that warms and inebriates' at the appropriate moment!"

In contrast, Sergeant Max Shortley, who was stationed at Newton from 1993 to 1998 in Air Traffic, witnessed the station's downsizing from a fully manned station to enclave status. His family's housing at Newton in the Airmen's Married Quarters (AMQs) was also disrupted by their eventual sale through Annington Homes. Max takes up the story;

"Having arrived from RAF Marham, Norfolk in September '93 under the premise that Newton would be closing within 18 months, I was initially disappointed to have to move into a room in the Sergeants Mess for 6 weeks whilst an AMQ became available. The wait however proved worthwhile as eventually Julia and I were allocated one of the best quarters on the estate, a three bedroom detached property on Friar Walk, normally reserved for someone of Warrant Officer rank. Our eldest daughter attended the nearby primary school, at St Peter's in East Bridgford and our youngest daughter attended the playgroup on camp. Julia became the school bus escort on the daily return journey to St Peter's before eventually becoming housekeeper to the Burt family who lived at the 'White House' in Newton. We considered the standard of accommodation very good and by far the best AMQ we had ever had, it was a real luxury to have both an upstairs and downstairs WC. Fixtures and fittings were reasonably modern, but the principal oddity was that the lounge had large double doors through to the dining room and clearly the builders had envisaged these being open all the time as there was no radiator in the lounge! Due to the layout of the room we had no choice but to close these doors and put our large dresser in front of them, consequently during the winter it could be a chilly room to occupy. The garden was of a good size and the children spent many happy hours playing in it. There did seem to be a rather convoluted drainage arrangement which joined all the houses in Friar Walk and we discovered one day that the manhole cover in the middle of our lawn was a key point as a blockage occurred somewhere nearby and we ended up with the sewage from about half a dozen houses bubbling up and flooding onto the lawn! We considered ourselves fortunate to have a small NAAFI shop nearby, otherwise everyday essentials had to come from either East Bridgford or Bingham. Thursday night was generally 'bratty' night as we used to get a mobile 'bratty' wagon site itself in a prominent place, trade was frequently brisk!"

"Once the station drew down to enclave status in 1995 we were briefed to expect a move onto camp to one of the older Junior Officer Married Quarters at Newton Gardens. The AMQ estate comprising Trenchard Close, Friar Walk and Fairway Crescent were to be handed over to 'Annington Homes' for subsequent disposal. The Non-Commissioned community had diminished significantly and what we thought would be an orderly move turned into a bit of a rush. We were concerned that we could end up being allocated what

was left if we didn't get our skates on, consequently we moved several months earlier than we had anticipated. However, it transpired that the rush wasn't really necessary as 'Annington Homes' took another 18 months to start the process of selling them off. We heard a story through the grapevine that they paid circa £15k for each property and when they eventually went on the market they were asking £45k for them, not a bad return for what amounted to little more than a lick of paint here and there! We had initially been interested in possibly purchasing our old house, however, it never came onto the market as we believe a 'closed door deal' may have been struck. In any case there was a subsidence problem which required extensive underpinning to the rear of the property, under the kitchen, so on our part it most probably worked out for the best!"

"The three bedroom semi-detached house we occupied at Newton Gardens was clearly in need of some modernisation, however, we ended up making do with a very ancient kitchen and bathroom, the overall size of the property was significantly larger and this too had a decent sized garden. We discovered early on that during the period between the Officers vacating these quarters and the Non-Commissioned community moving in there was initially a minor problem with rats in the area. They seemed to be able to find easy routes to and from the sewers through damaged drain covers etc. and could often be seen running around above ground in gardens, not ideal for families with young children! Another problem we struggled with was the rather ancient central heating boiler, which vented through the north facing kitchen wall, this was prone to having its pilot light blowing out whenever the wind was from that direction. Being ancient it simply refused to accept the recommended method of being re-lit, instead requiring the attention of a heating engineer complete with blow-lamp!"

"After a little over 4 years spent divided between these two properties and 17 years in total living in AMQs we decided that we liked the area enough to put down roots, eventually finding a very agreeable property in nearby Bingham. At the end of 1998 much to my great disappointment I was eventually prised out of Newton with a posting to Waddington. Of all the postings I had in over 24 years, none could compare with Newton and I will always have fond memories of my time there."

While a civilian community has established itself in the old Airmen's Married Quarters, giving these properties a new lease of life and a secured future, the former Officer's Married Quarters have faired less well becoming victim to vandalism (one was even burnt down circa 2005) and general deterioration. Had there not been the long-running uncertainty of the A46 road scheme possibly ploughing through this site, these large, once prestigious properties could have been sold off as an exclusive development and help relieve the nations housing shortage. The latest development came in April 2009 when work finally started on the A46 dualling and four properties were demolished. The rest will no doubt follow the same fate in due course and the area landscaped.

The former Airmen's Married Quarters in August 2008. T O'Brien

The Airmen's Married Quarters (AMQ) is sited outside the main gates. Overspill was in the former AMQs on Coney Grey Spinney, RAF Syerston.

Above: **1950s Airmen's houses on Fairway Crescent.** T O'Brien

Below: **The original 1930s AMQs on Trenchard Close as seen in 2008.** T O'Brien

Newton Gardens

Right: **'Air House'** was reserved for the highest ranking Officer. In latter years this was the **Air Commodore, AOC Air Training Corps.** T O'Brien

Below: **The Station Commanders house at 19 Newton Gardens, next door to 'Air House'.** T O'Brien

Bottom: **The wartime gymnasium sited at the end of Newton Gardens.** T O'Brien

Above: **One of the original 1930s style houses.** J Proudlock

Left: **A 1950s detached house.** T O'Brien

Below: **The semi-detached 1950s houses.** T O'Brien

BOROUGH OF RUSHCLIFFE

FREEDOM OF THE BOROUGH
CEREMONIAL PARADE

SALUS · POPULI

by

ROYAL AIR FORCE, NEWTON

on

FRIDAY, 23rd SEPTEMBER 1994

Councillor Mrs. J. M. E. Dixon, JP
Mayor,
Borough of Rushcliffe

Group Captain C. B. Adcock,
BA, FIMgt., RAF
Station Commander, RAF Newton

'Chain Gang' Days

RAF Newton always enjoyed good relations with the surrounding area by participating in local civic functions, plus Battle of Britain and Remembrance parades. In return the base hosted numerous visits by local dignitaries such as the Lord Mayor and Sheriff of Nottingham plus members of the Bingham Rural District Council who have been given guided tours of the station before dining in the officer's mess. Gp Capt Philip Langrill remembers these visits *"The annual 'Chain Gang' visit during which the many mayors, lord mayors, sheriffs, high sheriffs and other local dignitaries spent a day visiting the Station was always a great pleasure. Tradition demanded that they should be invited to the station once per year, wearing their chains of office! There were so many of them that the event had to be spread over two days! Several of the visitors told me that the 'Chain Gang Day' at Newton was the highlight of their mayoral year! Otherwise, the RAF Police Dog Championships invariably drew good crowds, which always included an impressive array of the top brass. They were always delightful occasions. So too, were the Battle of Britain Days which, although informal, proved very popular. We would start with a memorial service in the highly polished RAF Police hangar. There was always a sizeable crowd, many civilians from the local area were invited which swelled the congregation up to 800. The Nottinghamshire Police Band would accompany the hymns and I would read the lesson. A modest but impressive flying display would follow."*

The local Member of Parliament for the borough of Ruschcliffe and former Home Secretary and Chancellor of the Exchequer, the Rt Hon Kenneth Clarke, QC, MP remembers his contact with the base, *"I remember being a guest at the splendid, annual cocktail party. Newton maintained a reputation for holding the best party on the local civic circuit and they welcomed all leaders from various parts of the local community to a gathering in the mess. The various mayors and other local leaders were greeted, as my wife Gillian and I were, by very nice young officers, who escorted us round from group to group of distinguished guests chattering away over splendid quality drinks and canapés. It enabled me to try to keep up to date with the flow of officers and staff through the base and it left quite a gap in the social calendar when the base finally closed".*

On Thursday 14th September 1967 a reception was held in the Officers Mess at Newton, during which a lace panel, one of the famous Battle of Britain commemorative panels made in Nottingham was presented to the base for safe keeping. It was one of several produced by the Nottingham lace manufacturer Dobson and M Browne Ltd between 1942 and 1946. At 15 feet long and 65 inches wide it was accepted by the station commander Gp Capt E H Jenkins from Sqn Ldr (Retd), Councillor A Cave, Vice President of the Nottingham branch of the Royal Air Forces Association (RAFA). The panel was then displayed for public view whenever the station opened its gates to the local community from the 'Good Neighbour Day' in 1968 to the last Battle of Britain Open day in 1993.

Wednesday 15th April 1970 saw Newton receive the Freedom of the City of Nottingham. The granting of such Freedom confers on the Officer Commanding and all ranks the right, privilege, honour and distinction of marching through the streets of Nottingham on all ceremonial occasions with colours flying, swords drawn, bayonets fixed, drums beating and Bands playing. The civic ceremony was performed on the green at Nottingham Castle. Where the Lord Mayor, Alderman William Dyer handed over the prestigious deed granting the freedom to the station commander, Group Captain A Fry OBE. Following the ceremony twelve Jet Provosts from RAF Cranwell and five DH Chipmunks from East Midlands Universities Air Squadron then flew in formation overhead. Afterwards the 1000 uniformed members of the station led by the RAF's Southern Band paraded through the streets to enliven an otherwise dull morning. With the Drum Major throwing his mace up into the air, the airmen marched down Friar Lane and into the Old Market Square, where the Lord Mayor then took the salute outside the Council House. The second occasion that Newton exercised the freedom of the city was on 31st March 1979, when the Lord mayor of Nottingham presented a wooden crest depicting the city coat of arms to the station commander Gp Capt R G Bowyer AMBIM. Then after an absence of nearly a decade, the spectacle once again returned to the cities streets on 16th April 1988 in what was to turn out to be the last time the station would claim the freedom of the city.

Alderman, Mrs Anne Yates, chairman of Nottinghamshire County Council proved that she was always on top of her job, when on Friday 5th November 1971 she flew over the county in Chipmunk WG308 of EMUAS. Piloted by Sqn Ldr Robin Phipps OC EMUAS, she obtained an aerial view of Nottinghamshire including the proposed Alfreton to Mansfield growth areas. *"Although the bad weather made the flight bumpy, I gained a valuable look at these areas"* said Mrs Yates, who also added *"The purpose was to get a comprehensive view of the area which is impossible to obtain through maps."* The flight also included a close view of her work place at County Hall next to the Trent Bridge cricket ground, before returning to Newton via the National Water Sports Centre at Holme Pierrepont.

On 3rd May 1978, the station received a flying visit from Her Royal Highness Princess Anne, who arrived in a helicopter of the Queen's Flight. On arrival she was met by the station commander, Group Captain Tony Ferguson OBE her escort for the visit. Starting at 11 am with a tour of the School of Education, the Princess went on to visit the gymnasium hangar where she was greeted by the Physical Education Officer, Flt Lt Bill Dickson who introduced many live displays by station personnel. These included weight training, floor exercises and trampolining, as well as static displays of canoeing, mountaineering and camping. Whilst in here she also had the chance to chat informally to servicemen and their families. Local Scouts, Cub Scouts, Girl Guides and Brownies were also paraded before the Princess. After lunch, the Princess planted a Cedar Atlantica tree as a commemoration of her visit before being taken by limousine to watch a display by the Police dog handling section. Then to wind up the four-hour visit there was a brief tour of a static aircraft display comprising a Chipmunk, Bulldog and one of the new Slingsby Venture motor gliders based at Syerston. This also provided an opportunity for her to have a chat with glider pilot Flt Lt Peter Bullivant, who taught her brother Prince Andrew to glide in 1975 – 76. Despite the jubilation of all those who participated in the event, not everyone was happy with the visit. Local newspapers reported that a constituent had written to the local MP Kenneth Clarke demanding a breakdown of the cost to the taxpayer to 'smarten up' RAF Newton for the royal visit. However this was not to be the only visit by Royalty throughout Newton's history as one of the earliest recorded events was a visit on 11th June 1942 by Air Vice Marshal, His Royal Highness the Duke of Kent on behalf of the Inspectorate General.

During Sunday 11th March 1984, station personnel turned out for a parade in Southwell, providing a Guard of Honour and a flypast of four Bulldogs. The occasion was the rededication of the Airmen's Chapel in Southwell Minster, where a new altar rail was made and engraved by personnel in the station's workshops and a new silk RAF ensign displayed over the main altar. On 19th June that year a unique flypast of training aircraft took off from Newton and flew over the town, famous for the Bramley Apple. It included five aircraft; a yellow Tiger Moth T5493 from Cranwell, a Harvard from RAE Boscombe Down, a privately owned Provost XF690 flown by the station commander Gp Capt S Holding, a Chipmunk of 7 AEF and a Bulldog of EMUAS.

On 8th November 1984 Rushcliffe Borough Council unanimously decided to grant the Freedom of the Borough to the station in recognition of and confirming ties of friendly association, which had existed between the Borough and RAF Newton. The Freedom was then conferred at a ceremony held in West Bridgford on Friday 1st March 1985. This was to be a right the base exercised on three occasions, the second being on 3rd July 1990 until the last ceremonial parade on Friday 23rd September 1994 commenced at 10.35am. The parade comprised one squadron made up of two armed flights and one Flight of RAF Dog Handlers and their dogs with music provided by the RAF College band at Cranwell. A flypast of aircraft from 7 AEF accompanied the general salute taken by the Mayor of Rushcliffe at 11.33am before a lunch for the civic guests and Group Captain C B 'Sid' Adcock BA FMIGT, Newton's last station commander and the end of such civic functions.

"Tradition demanded that they should be invited to the station once per year, wearing their chains of office! There were so many of them that the event had to be spread over two days!"

Above: **Newton personnel meeting Civic leaders in Nottingham's Old Market Square; Battle of Britain week; 1952.** Author's collection

Left: **Seen in 2008, the Cedar Atlantica tree planted by Princess Anne in 1978.** T O'Brien

Opposite page:

Top left: **The Lord Mayor of Nottingham, Alderman W Derbyshire, the Sheriff of Nottingham, Councillor C M Reed and their ladies plus the Lord Mayor's Chaplain, Canon G Spittles pay a visit to Newton on 14th March 1966 and were greeted on arrival by the station commander, Gp Capt Jenkins and Mrs Jenkins.** Author's collection

Top right: **Visit by the Chairman of Bingham and district rural council, W A Moore JP, the Clerk to the Council and other members circa 1967.** Author's collection

Bottom left: **Alderman Mrs A Yates, the Chairman of Nottinghamshire County Council and Sqn Ldr Robin Phipps in Chipmunk WG308 prior to her flight on 5th November 1971.** Newton archives

Bottom right: **Chipmunk WG308 carrying Mrs Yates over County Hall, West Bridgford.** Newton archives

A BBC TV 'East Midlands Today' crew film the former No.9 SoTT Hunter F.2, WN901 on fire during the late 1970s.
Richard Harcourt

Sentinels of Newton

From 1945 onwards, Royal Air Force stations have taken part in the tradition of having a gate guardian. This was usually a redundant aircraft or military hardware picked at the station commander's discretion as having some relevance to the site. It also acted as a dramatic set piece to visitors entering through the main gate. For many years a Bloodhound Mk2 surface to air missile greeted visitors at Newton's main entrance representing the station's connection with missiles, and stood on the patch of ground at the side of the guardroom. The missile remained on gate guardian duties until circa 1974.

The Bloodhounds successor was Hawker Hunter F.1, WT694 that stood at the main gate for nearly twenty years to become a well-known landmark. The career of Newton's example started on 29th October 1954 with its first flight by the well-known company test pilot Hugh Merewether. Following its initial flight-testing the aircraft was issued on 2nd March 1955 to No.54 Squadron at RAF Odiham. Then in early 1956 following a spell with the Day Fighter Leaders School it moved to No.229 OCU, until its short flying career came to an end on 22nd November 1957. Given the maintenance serial of 7510M it was then used for instructional purposes at No.1 School of Technical Training at RAF Halton. When it ceased to be an effective training resource, WT694 entered the final phase of its military career to become a static display aircraft at RAF Debden in Essex. When Debden closed in 1975 and turned into army barracks, the Hunter left by road along with the Police School and depot for RAF Newton to take up a gate guardian role. In the early 1990s under the direction of the station commander Group Captain Philip Langrill who had actually flown with 54 Squadron's aerobatic team, the erroneous black and white chequerboard fighter band markings were repainted in Blue and Yellow to represent 54 Squadron. During 1995, as the station partially closed, WT694's time at Newton was up as well as its military career. It was sold off and transported by road to its new home at Caernarfon Air Museum in Wales. By coincidence after retiring from the RAF, Philip Langrill served for several years as the Curator of the Museum. *"One day I was astonished to find the component parts that belonged to the airframe of Newton's gate guardian lying on the grass beside the museum. It looked like the aftermath of a flying accident! The airframe had been bought by Air Atlantique, which was then operating Caernarfon airfield and it became the centrepiece of an exhibit which featured the development and history of the Hunter."*

Apart from the gate guardians there have also been a number of other static aircraft sited at Newton, acting like sentinels for the base. Although they have not strictly been display aircraft as they were mainly used for fire training exercises or by the Police dogs to detect contraband and explosives they became a feature of Newton's landscape. One of the best remembered is Vickers Varsity T.1 WL627 that stood on the dispersal point behind the Sergeants Mess. Designed as a replacement for the Wellington, the Varsity's presence was a poignant reminder of the stations past. WL627s final unit was No.6 Flying Training School at RAF Oakington and it was from here that she was flown into Newton in March 1976.

Right: **The Bloodhound missile that stood for many years by the Guardroom. This photo appeared on the station's Christmas card circa 1961/2.** M Blackman collection

Below right: **Hunter F.1, WT694, which served as gate guardian from 1975 to 1995.** T O'Brien

Bottom: **Vickers Varsity T.1, WL627 on the dispersal behind the Sergeants' Mess. At the time of its arrival, personnel found it difficult to order new stationary, but when the RAF Police put in a request for a redundant airframe for dog training, they were immediately offered a recently retired Britannia, Canberra or Varsity. Once they made their choice, the Varsity landed three days later, weeks before their order for felt pens arrived!** T O'Brien

Opposite page:

Upper: **Hunter F.2 WN901 ex-No.9 SoTT being set alight by the fire crews while a BBC TV 'East Midlands Today' team film them, late 1970s.** Richard Harcourt

Lower: **Fire out, the TV crew wearing high seventies fashion interview an officer for their programme.** Richard Harcourt

Here, the RAF Police Dog Training Flight used her, before departing in March 1989 to a company in Humberside. It has since been reported to have been scrapped with only the nose being saved. Others scattered around the base on dispersal points included a single seat Hunter, Hunter T.7 (both used for dog training and fire practice) and English Electric Canberra T.4 WJ867 that eventually moved on to Abingdon. For a time in the 1960s a derelict Chipmunk also stood next to the wooden hut belonging to 1936 Squadron of the Air Training Corps until being disposed of. However not all of these aircraft have been destined to be museum pieces or end up on the scrap heap. As the engineless English Electric Lightning T.5 XS451 (8503M), which was allocated to Newton's Engineering Training and Support Squadron in 1978 has since been restored to airworthy condition. This supersonic jet now graces the skies once more with other exiled classic jets in Cape Town, South Africa. In the end all these aircraft have contributed to the station's theme of teaching and learning as well as becoming features of the local landscape in their own right.

NEWTON COURIER

THE MAGAZINE OF RAF NEWTON   SEPTEMBER 1988

RESCUE

31 AG 59

To the Rescue

Above: **Featured on the cover of the September 1988 issue of the** *Newton Courier,* **the Hunter T.7 parked on the dispersal by Jubilee Plantation is used for crash, fire and rescue practice with the then new RIV (Rapid Intervention Vehicle).**

Above: **The fire crews dampen down a fire that had broken out in a prefabricated hut storing ammo boxes near Jubilee Plantation, circa 1962.** M Blackman collection

Below: **Fireman Mick Blackman stands by the fire tenders, a Land Rover 'Crash One' and a Thorneycroft Mark 5A, circa 1961.** M Blackman collection

Shadows from the Past

Looking up at the big sky above the grass runways, the sun descends in the west to leave an orange glow above Nottingham. The harvest moon and stars shine down onto the air cadets of 'A' flight reading a map during a night exercise around the old bomb dumps. Their task is to decipher the clues and find a hidden canister before cadets of 'B' flight do. Then, just as some silhouettes are seen diving into the old barn on the airfield's boundary the north wind starts to blow. Climbing the plateau from the valley below it snakes off towards the hangars, then out across the airfield again, which way does he want to go? Through the trees, before weaving around the concrete structures all night long, sometimes hiding in a doorway, then a rustle of leaves and splintered branches are strewn across the dark wet tarmac. Where does he go? Back to a hangar, startling the birds, echoes creak, the turn of a key the crack of a lock. A shining figure glides brightly past. What was this vision before you? With hairs standing on end, your blood runs cold as the creaking locks join flickering lights and echoes to bombard the hangar. Is it the wind, a startled bird in the rafters, the trees groaning outside or someone trying to get in?

Airfields would not be complete without their ghosts, shades of the past. Newton is no different with several reported happenings. In one of the barrack blocks and a hangar something unexplained decided to shatter the silence occasionally by opening and shutting doors and switch lights on and off! Others have heard the faint sound of 'swing' music and apparitions. But this was nothing compared to the Officer's Mess where stairs mysteriously creaked, lights flickered and doors would lock themselves shut. Lights kept going on and off in the East and West Wing for no apparent reason. Some say it could have been the revenge of a Mess Manager who hanged himself during the war. Even though I personally have never seen anything I can't help but feel a strange atmosphere in such surroundings, must be my Celtic superstitions! However I do know of people who have seen ghostly figures of airmen late at night. Perhaps we'll never know who they are as their shadows are doomed to eternally walk the airfield by the light of the bombers moon. Who knows?

For the worship of God there were several locations on the station. Located next to the Airmen's mess was the station church, which was dedicated by the Bishop of Southwell, the Right Reverend F R Barry DSO DD on 10th December 1944 after being built by station personnel. The structure was later used as the station cinema before demolition in 1964. In later years the Church of England Chapel could be found in building '59', the Community Centre and the Roman Catholic Church was located in what used to be the wartime parachute store opposite the water tower. However this wasn't the original location of the Catholic chapel. During wartime, as the only permanent place of worship was the Church of England building, Roman Catholic personnel used to convert the station gymnasium into a temporary chapel every Sunday morning. Ted Shuvalski remembers this chapel well, as he got married here in 1945 by a Polish priest after visiting Bingham

Church Parade

Lower right: **The station chapel interior, 1955.** Author's collection

Right: **The wartime parachute store that was used as the Roman Catholic church in the station's latter years. But from 1995, the Anglican church re-located here.** J Proudlock

Below: **A leaflet published in the early 1980s by the Naval, Military and Air Force Bible Society and given out to ATC cadets by the padre.** Author's collection

Bottom: **An oak gothic style table from the Anglican church at RAF Newton, with two Bibles given out to ATC cadets by the padre in the late 1980s.** T O'Brien

Registry Office. Following the ceremony, they walked a few yards to the old 'Fosse' Road and waited for a taxi to take them to the Midland Station in Nottingham. But when it didn't turn up they were invited to have a lift with some servicemen on a 'Queen Mary' lorry to the Station, from where they caught a train to their honeymoon destination of Southport.

There have been many station chaplains over the decades, but many may remember Rev Dorothy Twiss. One of a handful of female chaplains in the RAF who put a lot of time and energy into her job by visiting all sections of the base, including the ATC squadron and got to know everyone. By doing so, individuals were helped and difficult situations resolved peacefully, all benefiting from having Padre around. After retiring from the RAF in 1991, Dorothy Twiss moved south and became one of the first female ministers to be ordained into the Church of England.

The Church of England chapel had a choir that met and sang every Sunday morning. The Newton choir comprised of members of the forces, service families and a few from outside. One of the singers was Mrs Rosalyn Blackmore who sang with the choir for 10 years. Ros, whose late husband Oliver had been an RAF Fireman currently works at Newark Air Museum running the gift shop and recalls, *"With Ollie having been an RAF at Waddington you always continue to get involved with the RAF in one form or another. Once you've had a connection like that you never get rid of it, it stays with you and so as we lived at Bingham I joined the choir at the John the Baptist chapel, RAF Newton. I remember the padres were Tony Fletcher, Dermot MacKavana and Dorothy Twiss and the organist was Peter Smith. My children also sang with the choir as well as attending the Cubs, Brownies and ATC that also met on the camp. I suppose I was one of those who formed the core of the choir to keep the continuity going as others were posted away. There was also a good social life at the church, we would meet for coffee after church, organise BBQs, treasure hunts and trips to places like Rutland Water. Every March about 6 to 8 of us would travel from Newton to the RAF Chaplain Training College at Amport House in Hampshire for a weeks singing course. A chap called Paul Eddington-Wright used to teach us. You now see his name on the credits of Songs of Praise. It was such a shame when Newton closed".*

Servicemen who have been killed in the line of duty have had a tremendous impact on small rural communities surrounding airfields like Newton, as the locals also felt their loss when incidents occurred. In the tiny village of Shelford there are six military graves of airmen who died during the war. Two are RAF personnel, but four are from the Royal Australian Air Force. Three of these Australians perished in one crash. Their names are Sergeant John Leonard Allison RAAF aged 29 years from Warwick, Queensland, Sergeant Arthur H Stephens RAAF aged 31 from Mosman, New South Wales (NSW) and Sgt Edmund Hunt RAAF aged 20 from Rockdale NSW. All were from No.14 Operational Training Unit (OTU) and lost their lives as a result of an air operation near Gunthorpe Bridge on Tuesday 30th June 1942. As no technical failure could be found with the airframe during the crash investigation and with no eye-witness accounts, the exact circumstances of the tragedy have never been determined. What is known though is that they were on a night navigation exercise from RAF Saltby, Leicestershire a satellite station for

RAF Cottesmore, where the main bulk of 14 OTU was based. On that fateful night, the pilot was an Englishman, Sgt Robert Pierson of the RAF Volunteer Reserve, Sgt Allison was the Observer and the two Wireless Operators / Air Gunners on board were Sgt Stephens and Sgt Hunt. Their aircraft was a Handley Page Hampden Mk1, serial number AD802 (code GL-VI) and had attempted to land back at Saltby unsuccessfully, before going round again but in doing so had 'lost' the airfield. The flying accident report completed by personnel from RAF Newton concludes that whilst they were looking for a navigational pin point, the pilot must have lost control and at 0230 hours the aircraft spun uncontrollably and crashed vertically into a field near Gunthorpe bridge killing the four-man crew. The three Australians were then buried in Shelford, with the Rev A N Tribe, the station chaplain from Newton carrying out the service. The fourth member of the crew, Sgt R T Pierson aged 21 is buried in his home town of Carlton, Yorkshire at St Mary's Roman Catholic church.

The fourth Royal Australian Air Force headstone at Shelford is for Sergeant Richard Arthur Von Der Groeben RAAF, who died on 13th July 1942 aged 25. He was one of two bomb aimers in an Airspeed Oxford 1, V3874 belonging to No.1654 Heavy Conversion Unit, the other being Sgt J R Warren. That day Von Der Groeben's aircraft was returning back at low level down the Trent Valley to its base at RAF Wigsley in north Nottinghamshire after completing a high level bombing training flight over Clifton Pasture's range. The Oxford was seen to hit a tree near the Hall in Gunthorpe village at 1320 hours, killing the three-man crew. While Sgt Von Der Groeben was buried in Shelford on 16th July, Sgt Warren and the pilot Sgt Dobie were taken to the mortuary at RAF Newton pending their burial.

Out of the six Commonwealth War Graves at Shelford, the last two were stationed at Newton and died in a motorcycle accident. Their headstones read, Corporal E C Barley RAF, died 11th October 1941 aged 19 and Corporal R F Watson RAF, died 10th October 1941 aged 29. Even though they are all a long way from home, these graves are still visited by relatives and cared for regularly by local residents and the Commonwealth War Graves Commission so *"We will remember them"*.

Opposite page:

Top: **Nos. 1 & 2 Hangars, April 2002.**
T O'Brien

Bottom: **No.1 Hangar through the Poplar trees, April 2002.** T O'Brien

This page:

Left: **The grave of Sgt R A Von Der Groeben RAAF in Shelford churchyard.**
T O'Brien

'Newton Tower'

Newton's Control Tower is a classic concrete 'Expansion Period' Watch Office with Meteorological Section 'Villa'. It remained relatively unchanged externally apart from the original windows being replaced in the early 1980s and 'storm porches' added in the mid 1990s, which probably made it unique amongst other wartime operational RAF towers at the time by retaining its original appearance where others had Post-War Visual Control rooms added to the roof. Internally the layout was also still based on the wartime layout, although the control room was upgraded as technology advanced, most recently in 1997 with a modern grey metal console. Around the same time mono CCTV cameras were fitted to the hangars and a Portable Aerodrome Visual Control Room (PAVCR) that had previously been in use in the Falklands was installed in front of the tower to aid with the visual approach of aircraft to runways 25 and 31. This recycling process was commonplace with the closure and life of an RAF Station. Newton's Tower benefited from the closure of RAF Scampton in that it inherited quite a few pieces of equipment. The irony was that when Newton closed and Scampton re-opened, it got them back again plus some of the staff!

Max Shortley, a former Sergeant Air Traffic Controller and now a civilian MoD employee in Air Traffic at Scampton, remembers his posting to Newton from 1993 to October 1998.

"Controlling the visual circuit at Newton came as something of a shock for me having arrived from Marham where they had three squadrons of Tornados and a squadron of Victors. With only a relatively small grass airfield by comparison and a smaller and much slower fleet of aircraft in the Bulldog and Chipmunk and more latterly the Firefly, it was much, much busier than it had any right to be! It was very common to have 4 aircraft in the circuit with another joining and a queue forming at the hold for aircraft to depart! That said there was no real complexity to it, as it was much like 'shelling peas'! But just when you thought it was all going so well, someone would call "Fanstop" downwind and suddenly turn for the airfield which always necessitated a quick rethink of your circuit pattern and all the while you would be keeping a very close eye on the chap sitting in a tractor mowing right alongside your runway, with 6 grass runways there was always a lot of mowing going on! I think everyone was surprised when they published the tables of total aircraft 'movements' at all active RAF stations within the UK and Newton was sitting in 3rd position!"

"It was much, much busier than it had any right to be!"

This page:

Left: **An interior view circa 1987.**
T O'Brien

Below left: **The Portable Visual Control Room (PAVCR).**
Artist – T O'Brien GAvA

Bottom: **Newton's Tower in the early 1990s. Note the ATC cadets waiting outside the crew room enjoying the sunshine for their flight.** T O'Brien

Opposite page:

Top left: **A fine shot of the Tower in 1999.** J Proudlock

Top right: **A sign on the side of the Tower. GRSS stands for Ground Radio Servicing Station.** T O'Brien

Lower left: **Another comparison interior shot from circa 1987.** T O'Brien

Lower right: **The Tower interior in 1998. Note the new PAVCR out on the grass and the upgraded grey metal furniture and digital equipment.** Max Shortley

'Newton Ground'

A sequence of three aerial photographs taken by Cadet Warrant Officer T O'Brien from 7 AEF Chipmunk, WP984 on a dull 10th March 1991 as it circuits the airfield prior to landing.
T O'Brien

"It was very common to have four aircraft in the circuit with another joining and a queue forming at the hold for aircraft to depart!"

Former Newton resident, Firefly G-BUUE at its new home of nearby Tollerton.
T O'Brien

The Ministry of Noise!

Not everyone loved RAF Newton!

Living near to a working military airfield you would expect to put up with a degree of noise pollution from aircraft in the circuit, but for some even that was too much. The Nottingham Evening Post ran an article in April 1997 about the noise complaints from local villagers following the move to a seven-day-a-week flying programme, plus the arrival of the Joint Elementary Flying Training School and their yellow Fireflies, which saw Newton's flying activity increase to 8,000 hours a year. The newspaper interviewed a Mr Birkett of Bulcote, who said; *"RAF Newton is rapidly becoming the neighbour from hell. Normally the flying is from 9am to 5pm seven days a week and it's going to get worse without any avenue for complaint".* The MoD responded by suggesting residents note down the registration numbers of the individual aircraft and contact RAF Cranwell or the MoD low flying complaints line.

Even though the noise created by the Bulldogs and Fireflies could be shrill at times, the majority of people living in the vicinity appreciated having the Royal Air Force around, but following complaints from residents in the neighbouring villages of East Bridgford, Woodborough, Lambley and Epperstone, the aircrew had these villages circled in red marker pen on their charts as areas to avoid. Although this area to the North West of Newton was sometimes the only option they had as the aircraft needed to avoid the neighbouring air-space of East Midlands Airport and other military bases at Cottesmore, Waddington and Cranwell plus the gliding at Syerston and the parachuting at Langar. However, the protests didn't stop. Group Captain Sid Adcock recalls how he dealt with one complaint in 1994;

"On one occasion, in an effort to allay complaints about aircraft noise, we invited representatives from the local community to a briefing on the flying activities that took place on the Station. One of the visitors, who lived some ten miles north of the airfield, was particularly vocal, insisting that we regularly did aerobatics over his house. Unable to appease his evident wrath, I eventually invited him to come for a flight in a Bulldog. After some twenty minutes flying, and having given him more or less a standard ATC cadet sortie, we eventually arrived in the vicinity of his house, where I treated him to a few gentle aerobatics over some adjacent open fields. He was absolutely amazed at the distance we travelled in such a short space of time, and quickly came to appreciate that, although we did our best to avoid built-up areas and spread the noise as equitably as we could, it was simply not possible to avoid every home and hamlet in the area."

However the ultimate anti-noise protest took place in March 1996 when the Nottingham Evening Post also reported a story about how a Mr Quinn of Bingham breached security at Newton. Mr Quinn, who had retired from the Royal Navy through ill-health drove to Newton to complain in person about the increased flying activity. Unable to get past the guards at the main gate, he distracted them in order to speed off round the base. With the alarm raised, a chase got under way as he was pursued by military Land Rovers and the station fire engine. Eventually he was apprehended as he approached parked aircraft out on the pan by the RAF Police and escorted off the camp. Although this didn't stop his complaints until he eventually moved away from the area.

In the end, local villagers only had to put up with their 'neighbour from hell' for another three years before 'defence cuts' permanently silenced the skies over Newton for them.

Right and below: **Signage out on the perimeter track of the airfield, 2002.** T O'Brien

Opposite page:

The Buccaneers! A sailor enjoying the Buccaneer display at the 1989 'At Home' day. T O'Brien

**Bulldog XX623 (M) over the
Bingham Road playing fields
at Radcliffe-on-Trent, 1989.**
EMUAS collection

Tiger Moth DE978; NUAS, circa 1950.
L Hooton

Chipmunks of NUAS in formation.
EMUAS collection

The Green,
Green Grass of Newton

As the Tiger Moth biplane piloted by Squadron Leader Hugh F O'Neill DFC turned back towards Newton at a leisurely 81 miles an hour (mph), the peace was suddenly shattered by a DH Vampire jet fighter roaring past at 490 mph, followed by a 504 Sqn Spitfire XXII at 360 mph. They were taking part in a 45 mile air race that was the highlight of RAF Newton's Battle of Britain 'At Home' day on Saturday 17th September 1949. Newton was one of 82 airfields open to the public that weekend to celebrate the ninth anniversary of the Battle of Britain. After the opening ceremony by Mr Arthur Henderson, the Secretary of State for Air, a Tiger Moth piloted by Flt Lt D Giles DFC, thrilled the crowds with 'Balloon-bursting'. Other attractions included crazy flying, a flypast of six Lincoln bombers, a display by an Avon-engined Lancaster from Rolls-Royce and some action reminiscent of recent wartime days was provided by Harvards and DH Hornets strafing a dummy castle in the middle of the airfield. As well as the race, Hugh O'Neill took part in other events during the day, as he explains his involvement in the flour bombing display, *"Mrs O'Neill bought some bags of self-raising flour for my bomb aimer to use from the front seat of a Tiger Moth. An old 1912 Bull-nosed Morris was purchased in Nottingham and four bowler hatted occupants carried rifles while driving up and down the airfield as we tried to bomb them from the Tiger Moth, scoring at least one direct hit."* Then later in the afternoon he displayed the Meteor of 12 Group. The day culminated with a mass flypast made up of thirty-two aircraft over the airfield

RAF Newton's Battle of Britain 'At Home' days were an extremely popular local event for many years, enjoyed by both service personnel and public alike. Held on the nearest weekend to Battle of Britain day (15th Sept), they usually enjoyed good 'Indian Summer' weather with swarms of 'Daddy Long-Legs' dancing across the grass. It is most probably these events that the public will best remember Newton for. These annual air displays run by the Royal Air Force can trace their origins back to the aerial pageants held at Hendon in the 1920s and 1930s where Trenchard had the foresight to see their potential as a good public relations exercise. These events continued to thrill the crowds until the outbreak of war in 1939 brought them to a temporary halt. With their re-introduction after the war, they once again became an overnight success and started to grow in size and stature over the years. The numbers of RAF stations hosting these events also grew to include venues like Newton, which attracted huge crowds with people travelling by bicycle, coach, train and car from all over the county.

Those early post war years saw some spectacular displays and aircraft participants ranging from wartime Spitfires to the latest jet fighter. One of the highlights was the exhilarating air race, staged in 1949 and 1950. Sqn Ldr Hugh O'Neill, who was posted to 12 Group Headquarters on a three-year spell of staff work, relates a

For Your Infor

Foreword by

Air Vice Marshal
R. L. R. Atcherley
C.B., C.B.E., A.F.C.

Air Officer Commanding
No. 12 Fighter Group

as Clarks

CLEANERS · LAUNDERERS

ROYAL AIR FORCE
NEWTON

BATTLE OF BRITAIN
"AT HOME"

PROCEEDS TO
THE R.A.F. BENEVOLENT FUND

1952
SATURDAY
SEPTEMBER 20th

SOUVENIR PROGRAMME ONE SHILLING

TRY FORM

FOR AEROPLANE HEIGHT AND
SPEED JUDGING COMPETITION

R.A.F. NEWTON
"AT HOME"
18th September 1954

I estimate the height of the aircraft to be .... feet.

I estimate the speed of the aircraft to be .... mile . per hour.

Name ....
Address ....

This Entry Form should be handed in to the Information Kiosk (behind Flying Control) not later than 4 p.m. The correct or nearest to correct entry will be announced by .... 5 p.m.

ENTRY FEE 6d.

PLEASE HAVE CORRECT MONEY READY — WE ARE SHORT OF CHANGE

The R.A.F.'s Latest Swept-Wing Jet Fighters

Battle of Britain

THE ROYA
AIR FORC
at home
Saturday

story about how these air races at Newton came about. *"From time to time, the Group Air Staff, headed by the AOC would descend on the Nag's Head in the nearby village of Harby. The pub's landlord was Sqn Ldr Peter Field-Richards, who divided his time between running the pub and flight-testing for A V Roe at the adjacent airfield of Langar. These meetings would involve some serious darts matches, copious pints of beer and Colston Bassett Stilton cheese. With people in relaxed form, ideas started flowing for the 1950 'At Home' day. We discussed staging another headquarters air race and a ground and air attack on a tribal fort. I recall making a strong pitch for the race and as a result, for failing to keep my trap shut, I was instructed to organise and run the flying display, including the race. And so plans for the 1950 'At Home' began to take shape and we concentrated our minds on the air race."* They decided to use a 26½-mile triangular course, similar to the 1949 race. Newton's Maintenance Unit constructed two black and white chequered pylons and sited them on the airfields at Newton and Bottesford, with the third turning point being at Staythorpe Power Station, replacing Rampton Mental Hospital used in 1949. *"To advertise the big day on Saturday 16th September 1950, I well remember the effort made by Flt Lt David Giles, (PA to the AOC), who hung by his hands while fixing a poster to the nearby railway bridge over the Fosse Way".*

The final line up of resident and 'borrowed' aircraft included a Vampire I, Vampire V, Harvard, Anson XII, Anson XIX, Oxford, Spitfire XVI, Tempest V, Meteor IV, two Meteor VIIs, Beaufighter, Firefly and a Seafire. At one time, it was suggested that they invite Sqn Ldr Peter Field-Richards in an Avro York from Langar and Sqn Ldr Harvey Heyworth in the Rolls-Royce Avon engined Avro Lancastrian to participate in the race, but was soon abandoned as the thought of them mixing with the other aircraft at low level round pylons was too horrifying to contemplate. Instead, both aircraft carried out their usual display routine over the crowds. The Avro York piloted by Peter Field-Richards, featured three of the engines being shut down to demonstrate low flying on just one engine. An awesome sight as they crossed the airfield. However the stunt almost ended in disaster though when the engineer very nearly feathered the fourth engine by mistake when asked to restart the other three Merlin engines, *"A close shave indeed"* Peter recalled later.

Hugh O'Neill continues, *"I had flown in the 1949 race, but on this occasion, I thought it prudent to keep a beady eye on affairs from the control tower with the help of my colleague J B Wray. We sent the competitors away by R/T from the tower coupled with a wave of the chequered flag to add a traditional touch. As we saw the faster aeroplanes chase the slower machines, I had a momentary twinge that we had got carried away in the Nag's Head. For the race's mass finish, the aircraft arrived as a bunch with the odd straggler from east to west over the hangars at varying altitudes from low-level to, I suppose, about 500 feet. They were flying straight-and-level with strict orders to avoid any split-arse manoeuvres, as the expression had it, before dispersing with great care."* The finish was a David and Goliath affair with the winner being Flt Sgt R J Collins from Syerston in his Harvard, who forged ahead of the AOC in his Vampire at the last minute, to win the trophy and Air Vice Marshal G Harcourt-Smith receiving a whole Stilton cheese as second prize.

Above: **Avro Vulcan B.1, XA905 in No.2 Hangar during an open day with other No.9 SoTT airframes; Javelins and Hunters, plus model Se5.** Milan Petrovic collection

Below: **Vulcan XA905 circling Newton prior to landing on the grass runway on 14th September 1964.** Artist – T O'Brien GAvA

In addition to the Battle of Britain displays, Newton has also hosted other events for the benefit of the general public which included the Flying Training Command display held in 1953 and a series of 'Good Neighbour' days in the late 1960s. Another event was the Tri-Service 'Armed Forces' day that was held in the summer of 1984 as a recruiting drive for local schoolchildren. In the late 1970s and early 1980s an annual Christmas bazaar was held, at which the station opened its gates to the local community and gave the station a chance to raise funds for local charities.

During the 1980s and 1990s the Battle of Britain 'Open day' continued to be a stalwart in Newton's calendar of events. After the morning's church service held in a hangar, all the uniformed organisations paraded around the base, before the small but magnificent airshow got under way in the afternoon. The programme included everything from Tiger Moths and Spitfires through to the Nimrod and Vulcan. But for the 1987 and 1988 shows the highlight was two Harrier GR.3s from RAF Wittering that landed after their distinctive display and parked on the apron close to the public. This was all possible due to the Station Commander Group Captain R E Holliday with his connection to the Harrier force. These events continued to attract large crowds from the local community right up until the last display on 18th September 1994.

Apart from their participation at Newton's air displays, the Red Arrows also made welcome appearances over the base at other times of the year too. The RAF's premier aerobatic team used to practice their forthcoming display routine over the grass landing strip, much to the delight of the local residents.

Despite having grass runways with the main 25/07 at 3700 feet (1128m) long, 13/31 at 2300 feet (700m) and 01/19 at 2300 feet, Newton has seen some large aircraft land here over the years. Most recently in 1996 and 1997, when three RAF C-130 Hercules transport aircraft from RAF Lyneham operated out of Newton at low level for a few days, causing much local excitement. Although by the end of the second visit, the station wasn't as excited as they ploughed up a runway causing major repair work! On 14th September 1964 Newton received its largest visitor, when Vulcan B.1 XA905 of 230 OCU flew in from Finningley, which No.9 School of Technical Training then used for instructional purposes, before being sold for scrap on 29th January 1974. The same fate also awaited Avro Shackleton MR.3 WR990 of 120 Sqn, which eventually located a runway to land on during the hazy conditions of 17th October 1970, aided by the Fire Section laying out markers on the threshold. All in all it turned out to be an eventful last journey for during the flight from Kinloss, the pilot Sqn Ldr Colin Paterson and crew asked Midland Radar for a weather report on Newton. To which the controller responded by asking; *"where is it?"* – apparently he had never heard of it! However even in good weather, some pilots have found it difficult to find Newton's runways. In 1990, a long pause occurred in the flying programme of the annual Battle of Britain display. The silence only being broken by the commentator, announcing that an American A-10 was displaying above the concrete runways of Langar airfield, some five miles to the south!

The Final Lodgers

Top: **No.73 Royal Engineer Squadron (TA)** and one of their giant earth moving vehicles. The engineers would recreate bomb damage on the airfield before practicing how to repair the craters. It was rumoured at one time that dispersals would be constructed for Harriers from Wittering to be dispersed to Newton, but eventually came to nothing. John North

Above: **The joint Nottinghamshire and Derbyshire Police 'Squirrel' helicopter G-NMHS** was based temporarily at Newton in the late 1990s while its new base at Ripley was constructed. Max Shortley

Right: **Slingsby Firefly G-BUUE** of the Joint Elementary Flying Training School performing aerobatics over south Nottinghamshire, summer 1998. Artist – T O'Brien

On 6th January 1983, the continuing problem of the runways becoming water logged took its toll on a visiting aircraft. The victim was a visiting de Havilland Devon C.2 from RAF Northolt that got stuck in the mud and was eventually hauled free with the help of station personnel and a Land Rover. To rectify this problem there was always talk that an underground drainage system would have to be installed at some stage. Devons had been regular visitors to the airfield for thirty years transporting the AOC Training Group for the station's Annual Inspection, a job they performed until their retirement from the RAF in 1984. Other casual visitors included the Lynx helicopter from HMS *Nottingham* whenever the ship was in port and the vessels company paraded the Freedom of the City. Hot air balloons have also unexpectedly called in, mainly in the evenings as they ran out of wind.

It was from this same grass strip that I had my first taste of flying on 18th December 1983, when I went up in DH Chipmunk T.10 WP984 of No.7 Air Experience Flight (AEF). One of thirteen nationwide, the AEF was formed here in 1958 to give the cadets of the Air Training Corps (ATC), Combined Cadet Force (CCF) and local Air Scouts their first flying experiences. I can still remember that day, flying through the crisp winter sky observing the motionless smoke from distant power stations, before being allowed to take the controls for my first flying lesson. Even though I soon realised that I was not cut out to be a 'future pilot', opportunities like this were to provide me with plenty of inspiration for my aviation art. With every chance I had, I managed to take my sketchbook with me to record the day's activity with the ATC. This led me to meet many characters based at Newton such as Squadron Leader Bill Purchase MBE RAFVR, the CO of 7 AEF. After returning from Germany, he was posted to RAF Leeming as CO of 11 AEF and it was from here that he arrived at Newton to take command of 7 AEF on 16th November 1992, when Sqn Ldr Brian Jones retired. Bill compares Newton to other airfields that he has flown from, *"The beauty of Newton was that it had the classic wartime layout of three runways and was unique as being the last operational airfield in the RAF to have all grass runways. Although in winter when the ground became boggy, the wheels of the Chipmunk left more ruts in the runways than the Bulldog. But at least we didn't get the terrible smogs that the airfield experienced during the war, no doubt due to less pollution and less coal fires being burned"*.

An ex-39 Sqn Canberra pilot, Bill is also well known for his adventure in one of the two Chipmunks that took part in two attempts at a 'round the world' flight to celebrate the aircrafts 50th Anniversary. The aircraft had been modified to hold an extra fuel tank in the rear of the cockpit, which was designed under the supervision of Mike Haugh of Field aircraft before the aircraft left for fitting at Marshalls of Cambridge. The civilian firm of Field Aircraft, a member of Hunting PLC had the contract for many years to service the aircraft at Newton. The firm's Assistant General Manager for military business, Bob McLuckie closely monitored the project. After an aborted attempt in 1996 when they had to turn back due to enormous forest fires blocking their path in Siberia, they were determined to try again. The two aircraft accompanied by a Britten Norman Islander support aircraft, then set off for RAF Cranwell, from where their epic journey on 'Exercise

Northern Venture' began on May 20th 1997 and took them to Berlin, Warsaw, Russia, Alaska, Canada, Greenland before returning to Cranwell to much applause on July 21st after 64 days and 16,192 nautical miles.

From the cadet's point of view in the 1980s, not a lot had changed from Alan Sillitoe's flight forty years earlier. You still waited in the 'crew room' next to the control tower and the flights still lasted twenty to thirty minutes. With safety a priority, the aircrew briefed all cadets on what to do in an emergency and how to operate the parachute. This was backed up with the 'John Andrews' safety film for those who hadn't flown at all. Having been strapped up in the large bulky parachute, fitted with cloth headgear and bone dome you sat there waiting for your turn to fly. While other cadets played cards, read or chatted, it made you appreciate what it must have been like waiting for 'Scramble' during the Battle of Britain, how they ever managed to run wearing a parachute with those uncomfortable straps around your crotch, I'll never know! During foul weather it could be a dull wait though watching the same old videos, 'Iron Eagle', 'Under Siege' or the ubiquitous safety film in the main 7 AEF crew room located in the hangar annexe. All the time hoping that the conditions might improve and you could get your flight, only to be told at lunchtime that the wind, low cloud or rain wouldn't improve and you could all go home. But during a long summer day you might make up your losses by getting a second flight if you were lucky.

Not being able to hear anyone talking through your bone-dome it was difficult to assess if your aircraft had landed or not. But when your aircraft taxied across the grass, you would be taken out of the crew room by a staff cadet and led to the edge of the grass, waddling along with the cumbersome and sometimes crippling parachute. The Chipmunk would then taxi up to the tower, turn around and stop without the aid of chocks, relying instead on the aircraft's brakes. With the propeller idly chugging away, the staff cadet would run over to the aircraft from behind, climb onto the wing then open the canopy to un-strap the cadet. Once this cadet had been extricated from the cockpit and sent back to the crew room, you were beckoned to approach the rear of the aircraft, clamber in and sit down in the rear bucket seat, where the large parachute cushioned you. After being strapped in to the seat, followed by harness and intercom checks, the pilot released the brakes and you trundled off over the grass to the edge of the runway. With permission granted from the tower to take off, the Gypsy Major 8 engine burst into life, straining against the brakes. Once the brakes were released you were off. Bouncing along the grass you knew when the wheels had left the turf as you could feel the sensation of becoming airborne and seeing Newton and the surrounding area from a new perspective.

Looking at the back of the pilot's bone dome you often wondered what distinguished career your pilot had before flying you on this air experience flight. I remember one pilot wore a 617 Squadron patch on his flying suit and another had flown with the Red Arrows. While a lot of pilots had been on 'fighters', others such as Squadron Leader David Haller (Retd) and Group Captain John Laycock (Retd) had been 'bomber' men, both flying Vulcans with 44 Squadron from Waddington.

John had also been the Station Commander of Waddington and was involved in the 'Black Buck' raids on the Falklands. Whatever their former ranks all the pilots that fly with the AEF are ex-service or airline pilots and become 'Flying Officers' once again, under the command of a Squadron Leader.

During your flight, you often had the chance to fly over your home before climbing above the clouds and take control of the aircraft for a 'mini' flying lesson. David Haller recalls these lessons, "*It was a pleasure to fly the air cadets, many of whom had not flown before. The female cadets turned out to be generally better pilots than the lads when they took control of the aircraft*". After a few flights you could also participate in some aerobatics, depending on whether your stomach could take all those loops and barrel rolls. All before you could legally drive a car at the age of 17! But whatever you did during your flight, it always seemed to be over too soon as you descended over the Nottinghamshire countryside to approach the runway over the Trent valley. Having passed the derelict windmill you waited for the thud from the undercarriage coming into contact with terra firma again. As the Chipmunk swung round and stopped in front of the crew room like a taxi, you could see the staff cadet waiting with the next passenger. Waddling back to the building, it was a welcome relief to remove the sweaty headgear to breathe some fresh air and take off the bulky parachute, but quietly jubilant at having notched up another trip in a 'real' aeroplane.

However all this was to change with the retirement of the ageing Chipmunk in 1996 just short of its 50th Anniversary in service. As all the 'Chippys' from around the country were withdrawn, they were flown into Newton and stored in hangar No.3 pending the auction by Phillips in London in March 1997. Once sold, the buyers had to collect them direct from Newton. One new owner was the aviation artist Michael Turner, the President of the Guild of Aviation Artists who flew from Halton to collect his second example of the Chipmunk. "*I visited Newton in my other Chipmunk, WP800 on 6th February 1997 to view the lots. I had researched the lots in the sale and thought WP840 was a good one, the airframe and engine hours were not too high, the condition looked good, all the bits were there, a good complete example. On 13th March 1997 I took off from Halton in a PA28 with Ferry pilot Wing Commander Norman Trench, the Chairman of Halton Aeroplane Club to collect WP840. We arrived at Newton at 1300 hours in good weather, however unlike my first visit, the cloud shadows made the airfield difficult to spot. But we found it after a short detour as the shadows had moved on. The Chipmunk was in the hangar along with some others awaiting collection. The aircraft had been prepared for flight and checked over by Aircraft Restoration Company (ARCo) from Duxford. It now carried the civilian registration G-BXDM applied to the fuselage sides in black sticky tape. We took off at 1400 hours with the PA28 acting as the communications aircraft as the Chipmunk had no radio. We flew south to Corby and followed the motorway all the way to Duxford where ARCo carried out some CAA work before delivery to the RAF Halton Aeroplane Club who now own the aircraft and still operate it in the red, grey and white markings as it did when I obtained it.*"

As the Chipmunk was replaced in service with the Scottish Aviation Bulldog, stricter Health and Safety operating systems were also introduced. The aircraft now taxied to a halt on the apron, chocks and engines switched off plus a new slimmer parachute, bone domes and the inevitable increase in paperwork and risk assessments. Safer perhaps, but a much sanitised version of the real flying experience that had gone before! But that wasn't the only change, as part of the RAF's Training Structure all UAS and AEF's were also amalgamated during 1996, resulting in the University Air Squadron and the Air Experience Flight sharing the aircraft. Bill Purchase remembers the mood of the two units at the time, *"When the time came for us to merge with the UAS, naturally neither unit wanted to as we could see no advantage in it. I had five Chipmunks at the AEF compared with the four Bulldogs on the UAS, but after the merger we all ended up competing for reduced resources as the new unit had just six Bulldogs to go between us. But at least the future of the AEF and UAS was assured as many had thought that they might be axed altogether. And at least with the introduction of the Bulldog, we had gained side by side seating in the cockpit so the pilot could keep an eye on what the cadet was doing"*. As Newton had partially closed the previous year to become a detachment of Cranwell, the UAS and AEF had the airfield all to themselves apart from a handful of RAF Police that had remained. However the station was to be injected with new energy in 1997 when the Joint Elementary Flying Training School (Army Grading) arrived with their yellow and black Slingsby Firefly aircraft along with No.73 Royal Engineers Squadron (TA) and their large earth moving equipment and vehicles. Around the same time a 'Portable Aerodrome Visual Control Room' (PAVCR) was installed in front of the control tower and CCTV cameras installed on the hangars to aid with the visual approach of aircraft from a safety perspective. However as the MoD was investing again in Newton, it could only mean one thing, the dreaded C-word!

Newton had become the subject of gossip in the national housing crisis debate following the Government highlighting the need for millions of extra houses to be built across the country. As Newton is sited in a prime location in the affluent South Nottinghamshire area it seemed inevitable that it would be seen as an under utilised site and a candidate for a new housing scheme. So it was not surprising when in 2000 the decision was taken to finally close the site and transfer all flying to Cranwell as the MoD had decided that it was far too expensive to keep this "under used" site. Bill Purchase recalls the demise of Newton *"It was always difficult to see how they were going to keep it going after all the large lodger units like the Police, School of Education and HQ Air Cadets had left in 1995"*. However it was ironic that after all this time the MoD started to solve the problem of the runways becoming waterlogged. Circa 1998, the MoD spent a fortune on installing a new drainage system, which inserted gravel underneath the grass landing strip in a herringbone pattern. Bill remembers, *"During the scheme to install drainage, a tractor was damaged as it found some of the metal strip that was randomly scattered under the grass"* and another reportedly unearthed an unexploded bomb! Then in 2000 the remaining units prepared to depart. The departure to Cranwell for the UAS and AEF would also bring about another change with the retirement of the Bulldog and the introduction of the civilian owned and registered Grob Tutor.

The last day of flying at Newton for EMUAS and 7 AEF came on 25th August 2000. AEF pilot David Haller takes up the story. *"We had a great day, the weather was gorgeous and we had a BBQ and party. We flew a lot of people and even though we weren't allowed to fly in formation a lot of us flew a run-in and break. The atmosphere was jovial and we looked forward to the next stage at Cranwell, though we couldn't appreciate why we had to leave Newton, which was one of the few airfields that the RAF actually owned outright. The air traffic at Cranwell was also pretty heavy what with Dominies, Jetstreams, the Red Arrows and a private flying club! Newton was a delightful airfield to fly from as the grass was generally flat and level and we had the place all to ourselves, it was almost like a 'Professional Gentlemen's Flying Club'. As a flying unit we had an excellent safety record with very few incidents, no crashes or bail-outs".* Having left Newton, the move to Cranwell unfortunately did not run smoothly at all, as the new building wasn't ready. This meant that the AEF was not able to fly any cadets for about six months until all the difficulties of moving had been ironed out. As the Commanding Officer of No.7 AEF, Bill Purchase finally flew out of Newton for the last time on the 3rd September 2000. By October 2000, the UAS and AEF had fully moved over to Cranwell, followed by JEFTS who moved to Barkston Heath and Middle Wallop. By November 29th when the tower closed all flying had ceased over Newton.

Looking back AEF pilot John Laycock remembers the green, green grass of Newton with affection, *"For me Newton was unique as you always had three serviceable runways based on the old wartime system at your disposal compared with just the one at other more modern stations. Also you had the control of your own air-space, it was just us at Newton unlike Cranwell that is so busy. Being so close to Nottingham, I always enjoyed flying the cadets over the city and the weather was generally better in Nottinghamshire than at Cranwell. And compared to all the maintenance needed for concrete runways at other bases, the only maintenance needed for the grass landing strip at Newton was a lawn mower!"*

A 7 AEF Chipmunk taxies back to the Tower. T O'Brien

Visitors

In addition to the resident Chipmunks and Bulldogs, Newton played host to a wide variety of visiting aircraft.

Top left: **An RAF Chinook spent a few days lifting loads from the southern side of the airfield circa 1997.** Max Shortley

Top right: **An RAF Devon gets stuck in the mud on 6th January 1983 after bringing the AOC for his annual inspection.** Newton archives

Upper right: **Aces High! You could be forgiven for thinking you were on the Western Front in 1917, but this is in fact one of a trio of SE5 replicas that stopped at Newton for a few hours en route to their destination.** Max Shortley

Lower and bottom right: **Two photographs taken from the tower by Sgt Max Shortley of two RAF Hercules during their first deployment in 1996. The aircraft were assessed as being too heavy for the concrete apron, so spent the night under armed guard on the grass instead.** Max Shortley

Left: **A Westland Whirlwind delivers Alderman Mrs Ann Yates JP, LMRSH, Chairman of Nottinghamshire County Council for her visit to the Newton during Battle of Britain week, 1968.** Author's collection

Below: **An impressive line-up of Chipmunk, Messenger, Auster, Prentice and two Wessex for the last 'Air-Day'; 1994.** T O'Brien

Bottom: **A Grob Vigilant from 644 VGS; Syerston at the 1993 Air Day.** J North

Maintenance

This page:

Top left: **ATC Cadets being strapped into their parachutes by personnel from Hunting.** T O'Brien

Top right: **An engine test on a Firefly by the old MT car wash.** Barrie Widdowson collection

Above: **A Chipmunk and tool rack; No.2 Hangar.** T O'Brien

Opposite page:

Top: **Servicing a BBMF Chipmunk and EMUAS Bulldog.** T O'Brien

Lower right: **Routine maintenance on a Chipmunk in No.2 Hangar, 1994.** T O'Brien

Bottom right: **Chipmunk being refuelled, 1994.** T O'Brien

Bottom left: **A painting commissioned by Bob McLuckie, the Manager of Field Aircraft.** Artist – T O'Brien GAvA

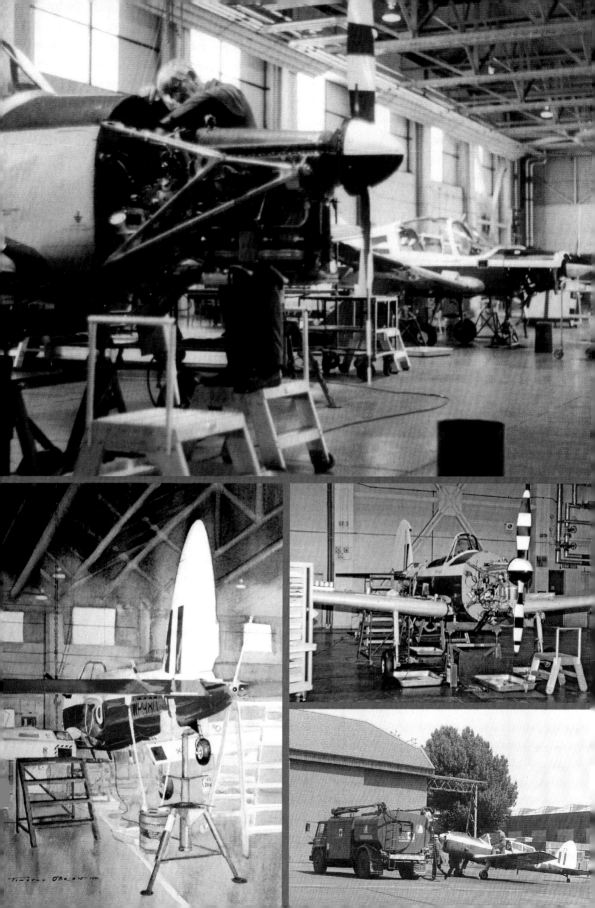

'Climb In!'

A painting by T O'Brien titled 'Climb in!' of a 1211 Swadlincote Sqn cadet about the climb into a 7 AEF Chipmunk in the early 1970s.

7AEF

FIRE EXIT
KEEP CLEAR

7 AEF

Opposite page:

The fire escape door to the 7 AEF room in the annexe buildings of No.2 Hangar.
T O'Brien

This page:

Top left: **Chipmunk taxying out under the direction of a Huntings member of staff.** T O'Brien

Left: **A Bulldog fires up at the start of an Air Experience Flight, 1997.** T O'Brien

Below: **A redundant Chipmunk used as a simulator, 1991.**
T O'Brien

Bottom: **Bulldogs waiting for trade on a Sunday morning, 1997.**
T O'Brien

Opposite page:

Top: **A painting by Timothy O'Brien GAvA called 'A first flight' features an ATC cadet climbing into a Chipmunk for their first air experience.**

Left: **A changeover of cadets in a Chipmunk, 1994.**
T O'Brien

Right: **Sqn Ldr Bill Purchase by Chipmunk WP833.**
T O'Brien

This page:

Left: **A painting by the author of a 7 AEF Chipmunk which was commissioned by Sqn Ldr Purchase and produced as a print and sold to cadets as a souvenir of their flight.**
Artist – T O'Brien

Below: **The two Chipmunks in front of the tower prior to their 'Round the World' flight in 1996.** Max Shortley

FIRST FOLD

- - - - - - - - - - - - - - - - - - -

BAG, AIR SICKNESS NATO STOCK No 8105-99-130-2180

SECOND FOLD

- - - - - - - - - - - - - - - - - - -

CLOSE BY FOLDING ONCE
TOWARDS YOU, PEEL RELEASE
PAPER FROM PANEL, FOLD AGAIN
AND SECURE.

This page:

Above: **The change-over of cadets between flights in the Bulldog. See the Chipmunk change-over on the previous page for a comparison of the old ways before 'Health & Safety' took over.** T O'Brien

Right: **Cadet Phil George of 1936 Sqn becomes the first of the squadron cadets to sample a flight in the Bulldog.** T O'Brien

Lower right: **Out with the old and in with the new! A Bulldog waits on the pan for a Chipmunk to return to the hangar.** T O'Brien

Opposite page:

An un-used NATO Standard sick bag! Author's collection

Air Displays

Main picture: **An impressive line-up for the 1952 'At Home' day. From left to right are a Vickers Varsity, Boeing Washington and Avro Lincoln while a Percival Prentice flies overhead. In the distance is a row of Meteors and behind the Washington is a Harvard and a Supermarine Attacker.** Author's collection

Opposite page:

Top: **A Tiger Moth from NUAS, Martinet, Prentice, Mosquito, Spitfire, Meteor, Auster and two Oxfords at the 1949 'At Home' display.** via H F O'Neill collection

Left: **Bristol Brigands attack the mock fort during the 1950 'At Home' display.** via H F O'Neill collection

Right: **An engine test-bed Avro Lancaster from Hucknall makes a low pass over the crowd at the 1950 'At Home' display.** via H F O'Neill

Air Vice Marshal
G. Harcourt-Smith
C.B., C.B.E., M.V.O.

Air Officer Commanding

No. 12 Fighter Group

WE welcome you to Newton today as guests of No. 12 Fighter Group, we hope you will find your visit enjoyable and interesting.

Ten years ago the Squadrons of Fighter Command fought out over these Islands one of the most decisive battles in history. It is that—The Battle of Britain—which the Royal Air Force commemorates this week and today most R.A.F Stations are At Home to visitors, as we are to you.

This afternoon you will see something of the work which goes on and some of the equipment used to ensure that the fighter defences are ready should this country be attacked again.

Welcome to Royal Air Force, Newton and a happy afternoon to you all.

Air Officer Commanding
No 12 Fighter Group

Opposite page: **The welcome page from the 1950 programme.** H F O'Neill collection

Right: **A plan of the station from the 1950 programme.** H F O'Neill collection

Below: **A badge for the AOC's enclosure.** H F O'Neill collection

Bottom: **Flt Sgt R J Collins receives his prize of a model Hurricane (borrowed from the Officers Mess) from the wife of the AOC, Mrs Harcourt-Smith.** H F O'Neill collection

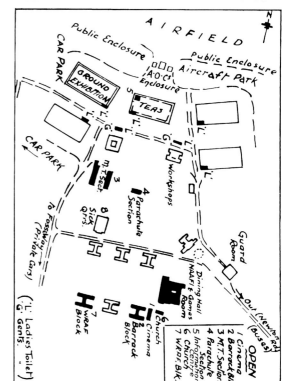

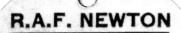

R.A.F. NEWTON

BATTLE OF BRITAIN

16TH SEPTEMBER, 1950

A.O.C.'s

ENCLOSURE

THIS BADGE SHOULD BE WORN

Opposite page:

Top: **DH Hornets at an early post-war display circa 1947.**
Author's collection

Centre: **The 1954 'At Home' day on Saturday 18th September looking South-East towards the range. Aircraft include a Vickers Varsity and an RCAF Beech UC-45 from Langar, a Provost, Boulton Paul Ballilol, Anson and a line-up of Meteors.**
Author's collection

This page:

Top right: **An enthusiastic crowd for the 1949 display.**
via H F O'Neill collection

Upper right: **A Bren Carrier at the 1949 display.**
via H F O'Neill collection

Lower right: **A Harvard and Sea Fury from nearby Syerston at the 1949 display.**
via H F O'Neill collection

Below: **An impressive line up of aircraft from Flying Training Command and Fighter Command in the static display, 1953.** Author's collection

Top: **Provost XF690, often piloted
by former station commander,
the late Gp Capt Steve Holding.**
T O'Brien

Above left: **The Red Arrows.**
T O'Brien

Above right: **A Percival Prentice at
the final 'At Home' day, 1994. A
pleasant reminder of the 22 FTS
examples that used Newton for
'circuits and bumps' in the early
1950s.** T O'Brien

Right: **A Harrier at the 1988
'At Home' display.** T O'Brien

Top: **Avro Lincoln and Avro Anson in formation circa 1947.** Note that far right, the wooden structure of the old derelict windwill is still standing – just! Author's collection

Bottom: **The Flying Training Command display, 1954 which featured a Vickers Varsity, Bristol Brigand, Chipmunk, Kirby Cadet III and Sedburgh glider in the static display. Note the steam rising from a passing train.** Author's collection

Parades

Opposite page, top: **Personnel from HQ 12 Group explain the workings of their Vampire to the general public in Nottingham's Old Market Square, late 1940s.** Author's collection

Opposite page, bottom: **The 1965 Battle of Britain parade enters the Old Market Square, Nottingham from King Street to pass Alderman Derbyshire taking the salute in front of the Council House.** Author's collection

Below: **Personnel from Newton enter Southwell Minster for the 1945 Battle of Britain commemoration.** Author's collection

Bottom left: **The morning church service in Two Hangar during the 1985 Battle of Britain 'At Home' day. The Battle of Britain Lace panel hangs behind the altar and flanked by a Chipmunk and Bulldog.** 1936 Sqn collection

Bottom right: **ATC Cadets from 1936 Squadron with their standard during the 1991 'At Home' day Battle of Britain parade.** J North

'Air Training over the Trent'

A painting by Tim O'Brien of a 7 AEF Chipmunk over the railway viaduct at Radcliffe-on-Trent. The large plume of Fumulus cloud in the distance has risen from the coal-fired power station at Ratcliffe-on-Soar.

Farewell

In the weeks following the official closure on 1st March 2001 the Royal Engineers finally departed with the last of their earth moving equipment. Rumours then circulated that English Heritage were looking at preserving the former RAF site as one of the few classic examples of a pre war 'expansion period' airfield left intact. This was soon followed by another about a television company purchasing the site for a massive studio. That is until 2002, when the Home Office selected the 39-acre site around the Officer's Mess and Quarters amongst other redundant military sites as part of its strategy to tackle the growing problem of Asylum Seekers and illegal immigrants entering Britain.

These plans were overwhelming rejected by local residents, refugee groups, Rushcliffe Borough Council, and the House of Lords. Meanwhile plans for the site at Throckmorton in Worcestershire were shelved while the site at Bicester in Oxfordshire was given the green light, even though a planning inspector had rejected the scheme at their public enquiry. Another site at the former HMS *Daedalus* at Lee-on-Solent on the south coast was selected in 2003 before that too was deemed unsuitable in early 2004. Despite a public enquiry into the suitability of the 'green belt' Newton site, the Home Office voiced their determination to press ahead. At the same time, the once shelved scheme to upgrade the A46 into a dual carriageway also re-emerged for consultation. Then on 7th July 2004, the deputy Prime Minister, John Prescott quietly announced that he had dropped plans for the Asylum Seeker Centre at Newton and the whole site would be sold. The plans at Bicester were also discreetly cancelled in June 2005 bringing a close to this failed and costly Government scheme. One side-effect of this period of indecisiveness over the site was that vandals infiltrated the Station to start the demolition process before a more effective security firm was employed as a deterrent.

The sale of the 595-acre site at Newton by the Defence Estates was then completed in early 2005 to a consortium of property developers called 'Newton Nottingham LLP', with a view to developing the 'Newton Forty-Six Business Park', a mix of housing and work units. This involves demolishing most of the technical site and living quarters, but will retain the old stores, wartime armoury, workshops, hangars and control tower, which had already been leased to commercial occupants in late 2007 and re-painted light grey to signify their protection from the JCB in the short-term. However, 200 acres around the Dawson's and Jubilee Plantations and bomb dumps were supposed to revert back to the Crown Estate under ancient historical rights, but at the time of writing (August 2008) were still owned by Defence Estates (MoD), although the runways are being leased back to local farmers who had land taken away during the late 1930s. In December 2007, 'Newton Nottingham LLP' were granted outline planning consent to build 164 houses. Demolition contractors were then brought in to quote on how much to raise the site. During March 2008, after eight years of appealing to the Borough Council, Shelford and Newton Parish Council finally got the main road up through the Airmen's Married Quarters named 'Wellington Avenue'. However their request to the landowners to save the main gates as a memorial to Royal Air Force Newton, looked doubtful especially as a new twist in the saga emerged in the press during April 2008. Local newspapers reported that the Government had pinpointed Newton as the Nottinghamshire site for one of its new eco-towns of 6000 properties, which seems to have overridden previous plans and would see the demolition of the Hangars and Control Tower. Again, as with all former ideas the controversial eco-town was greeted with caution as the local infrastructure had still not been upgraded to cope with such a scheme. So, the seemingly never-ending saga over what to do with the site continues and the station buildings were still standing during July 2009 as the country headed from the effects of the 'Credit Crunch' into a full-blown economic 'recession'.

As the air of transition continues to blow around the huge green hangars and water tower that still dominate the rural landscape, grazing sheep have replaced aircraft on the grass runways, while the wild rabbit population and hovering Kestrels have increased to create a haven of wildlife. Since 2001, a variety of businesses have operated from the site on short leases to keep the site 'alive' until a positive conclusion is reached. These have included a motorcycle training school and marquee company. Airliners now fly into the old airspace waiting to land at East Midlands Airport. Television companies temporarily employ No.2 Hangar to film programmes such as 'Jungle Run' and the cult 'Robot Wars' series, while an episode of 'Bad Girls' was filmed in the Officer's Mess and director Shane Meadows filmed parts of 'This is England' around the OMQs. For a short time, civilian dogs of the Drugs and Explosives Search Association (DESA) utilised the old dog kennels and training areas until being forced to close under dubious circumstances. Civilian police now based in the wartime armoury also use the site for riot training with horses and dogs, while No.1 Hangar is now occupied by a communications construction firm called 'EVE', part of the Babcock Group. Other hangars are employed as large storage facilities, while the Control Tower awaits a tenant. In April 2009 Balfour Beatty occupied the Station Headquarters and constructed workers accommodation units and a heavy plant park near the Sergeant's Mess for the three-year A46 dualling scheme.

Occasionally the military make a welcome return when they fly overhead using Newton as a navigational aid. Otherwise the former Royal Air Force station has joined 'Margidunum' in the history books. This just leaves 1936 (Newton) Squadron of the Air Training Corps located in their converted NAAFI shop by the main gate, as the only permanent remaining link to military times.

Since the closure, many people have returned to pay their last respects to what they knew as RAF Newton. While most arrive by car, bicycle or on foot, 7 AEF pilot John Laycock returned appropriately by air to fly over Newton one last time in a Grob Tutor before his retirement in August 2003. John *recalls "One of our staff cadets Simon Brown, who is also a member of 1936 Newton Sqn asked if we had enough time to fly over to Newton one afternoon to have one last look at the base from the air. As we approached the airfield we were amazed at how quickly the runways had disappeared under the grass, where had they gone?"*

When I asked the former Station Commander, Gp Capt Philip Langrill if he had ever been back since he retired in 1993, he replied, "*I have only been back once. That was to attend the final Officers' Mess dining-in night, which was also attended by Gp Capt John Martin. I have passed the place from time to time and always look out for the Poplar trees, which stand at the bottom of 19 Newton Garden's back garden. I never take a close look because I am content to remember the place as it was; busy, vibrant, friendly and efficient. The closure of RAF Newton, where excellent instruction was provided at modest cost, seemed to be an almost offhand gesture, symptomatic of the general decline and dimunition of our flying service*".

When I met Stan Wright at the guardroom back in August 2003 it was his first proper look round the base since 1942 apart from a brief visit during the early 1980s to chop down some trees down near the Officer's Mess that had 'Dutch Elm Disease'. The first thing to strike Stan is, "*Where have all the trees gone. I remember planting most of the poplars sixty years ago. Oh look there we are, that tree stump is from one I planted by this hangar back in 1938*". As we stand on the wet apron looking out over the airfield the BBMF Dakota appears again out of the gloom to head off over the Trent Valley past the old windmill. Then as another roar from the crowd watching 'Robot Wars' echoes out of the hangar behind us Stan takes a nostalgic view, "*If only we could turn the clock back? What I would really like to see is a row of Wellingtons sitting on the grass over there, just as I saw them all those years ago*".

For many individuals, RAF Newton has influenced their lives for better or for worse. Some were posted here from far away. Some loved the uncomplicated and relaxed nature of the station, while others hated it for various personal reasons. Many fell in love during their posting and settled here, some were born here, raised here and some died here. Then for others it was just a temporary home during a short posting or National Service, but whatever their recollections, the base has had an impact on their lives. The surrounding rural community has also felt its presence in many ways and mourns its passing like an old friend of a bygone age. For me, RAF Newton has been a significant part of my life too. By revisiting the site several times since the closure and talking to others more closely associated has helped me gain a better understanding of the birth, life and death of the station. Which has empowered me to write this history, which I hope has gone some way towards preserving its military past. So, looking to the future, as the sad, but inevitable march of progress is moving the site in a new direction, I feel that it is finally time for me to let go, bid farewell and remember Royal Air Force Newton with fond memories.

"I never take a close look as
I am content to remember the
place as it was, busy, vibrant,
friendly and efficient"

RAF Newton today. Photographed on 8th August 2008 from Firefly G-BUUE.
What does the future hold for the site? T O'Brien

The Times, they are a Changing!

Top: **Temporary accommodation for the A46 road builders. Note Building 39 that is now inside the compound.** T O'Brien

Left and below: **Construction of the heavy plant park next to No.5 Hangar; 2nd July 2009.** T O'Brien

Chronology

1936   Construction begins at Newton.

1939   Airfield opens for emergency use. 49 & 83 Sqn Hampdens dispersed here.

1940   July 3rd – RAF Newton officially opens. 103 & 150 Sqns arrive.

1941   103 & 150 Sqns depart. No.16 (Polish) SFTS arrive. NUAS formed.

1942   1936 Sqn Air Training Corps formed.

1946   16 (Polish) FTS disbands.

1947   12 Group HQ arrives.

1957   7 AEF formed.

1958   12 Group HQ depart for Horsham St Faith.

1959   No.9 School of Technical Training arrives.

1973   No.9 School of Technical Training closes.

1974   School of Education arrives. NUAS renamed EMUAS.

1975   HQ Air Cadets / RAF Police and dogs arrive.

1995   Newton reduced to enclave status. HQ AC / RAF Police & dogs / SOETS depart.

1997   Joint Elementary Flying Training School Firefly aircraft arrive.

1998   No.73 Royal Engineer Squadron (TA) arrives.

2000   JEFTS, Royal Engineers, EMUAS, 7 AEF depart. Airfield closes.

2001   March 31st – RAF Newton officially closes.

Above: **The tower after heavy snows, mid 1990s.** Max Shortley

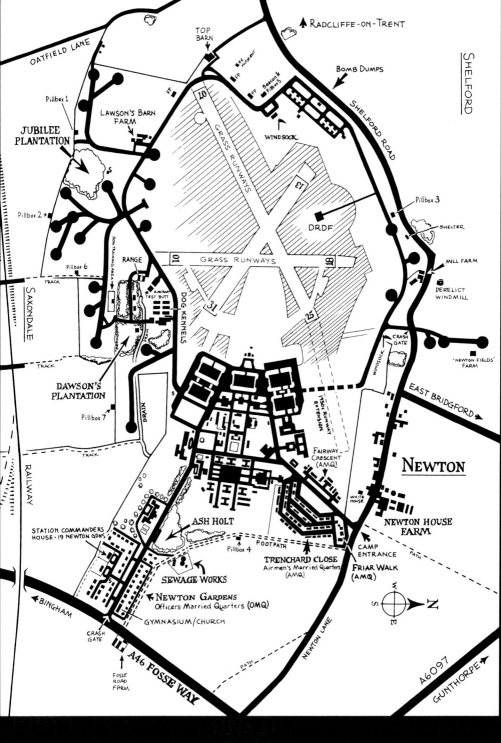

Plan A

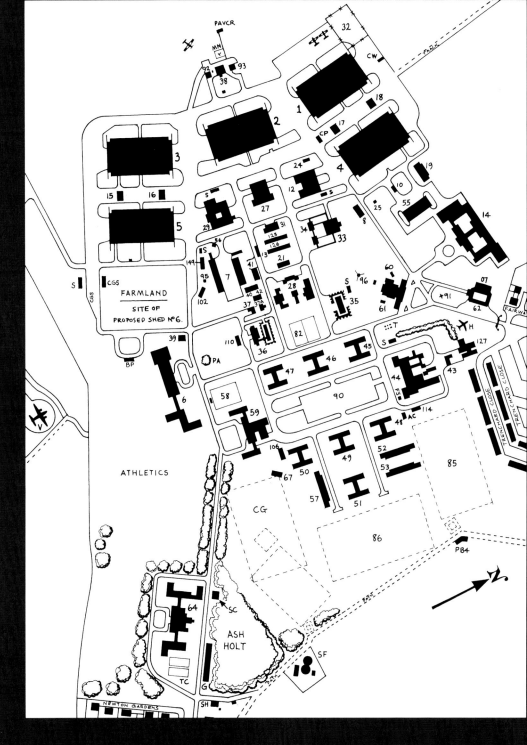

Plan B

Key to Plans

A key to the 'Building numbers' and codes on the accompanying plans A and B, which correspond to the actual numbers assigned to the station structures. These also served as a quick reference guide for the Fire section and RAF Police in case of an emergency or security situation. However, there are some buildings such as 37a that were always verbally referred to as 'Building 15', but does not appear to have a number assigned on any known plans. If you have the answer, please contact the author.

1	Shed No.1 'C' Type Hangar (Protected).
2	Shed No.2 'C' Type Hangar (Protected).
3	Shed No.3 'C' Type Hangar (Protected).
4	Shed No.4 'C' Type Hangar (Protected).
5	Shed No.5 'C' Type Hangar (Protected).
6	Sergeant's Mess, 1962-1995.
	Combined Mess, 1995-2000.
7	Mechanical Transport (MT Sheds and Offices).
8	Wartime 'Link Trainer' building.
	Postwar use as a model club HQ.
10	Bulk Petrol Storage installation. 6 x Underground tanks.
12	Station Workshops.
13	Articulated trailer shed.
14	Educational block, built 1961.
15	4 Bay Petrol tanker shed.
16	4 Bay Petrol tanker shed.
17	4 Bay Petrol tanker shed.
18	4 Bay Petrol tanker shed.
19	Postwar Boiler House, constructed circa 1961.
21	Wartime 'Parachute store'.
	Roman Catholic Church to 1995, then Anglican from 1995-2000.
24	Wartime air raid shelter, 'Stanton' type.
25	Pyrotechnic store (Flares etc).
27	Wartime 'Armoury'.
	Station Headquarters, 1947-1957.
	Regional printing centre and Photographic section, 1975-1995.
	HQ 1936 Sqn ATC, 1996-2000.
28	Water Tower.
	Wartime 'Works Services', 'Contractors Yard', 'Sub Station' and 'Gas Defence'.
29	Stores. Postwar 'Supply Flight'.
31	Lubricants and Inflammable Oil Store.
32	Missile compound 1961 to 1987. MT Yard, circa 1988 to 1995.
33	Wartime 'Central Heating Station'.
	Postwar Compound Yard.
34	Wartime 'Central Heating Station'.
	Postwar Compound Yard.

35	Wartime decontamination centre (*unwounded*). Postwar Defence Operations Centre (*in times of emergency*). Also used for NBC training.
36	Station Sick Quarters (later renamed 'Medical Centre') with annexe.
37	Wartime Mortuary and Ambulance Garage. Oxygen store.
37a	Wartime 'Disinfector Boiler House'.
	Postwar PSA Staff building.
	1936 Sqn ATC annexe, 1980s/90s.
38	Watch Office with Meteorological Section 'Villa'.
39	Wartime use un-confirmed, but could possibly have been used for Gas Defence training or as an overspill gaol for the guardroom.
	Farm shop, 1950s.
	Photography club, 1980s.
	ATC Radio hut, 1990s.
40	Wartime timber hutting. Demolished early 1990s.
	Postwar use as accommodation for ATC Cadets on gliding courses at Syerston.
41	Wartime timber hutting housing the National Westminster Bank. Rebuilt late 1980s in brick to house PSA Staff before privatisation.
42	Wartime timber hutting. Demolished early 1990s.
43	Wartime 'Ration Store'. Postwar 'Station Catering Flight'.
44	Institute (Fosse Club & Airmen's Mess (Dining rooms).
45	Barrack 'H' block 1. RAF Police museum, 1975-1995.
46	Barrack 'H' block 2. Headquarters Air Cadets, 1975-1995.
47	Barrack 'H' block 3.
48	Barrack 'H' block 6.
49	Barrack 'H' block 5.
50	Barrack 'H' block 4.
51	Barrack 'H' block 7.
52	Barrack block built 1961/2.
53	Barrack block built 1961/2.
55	Wartime MT Storage Shed.
56	MT Section guard house.
57	Barrack block built early 1980s.
58	Tennis Courts.
59	Sergeants Mess, 1940-1962.
	Community Centre and CofE Church, 1962-1995.
60	Station HQ outbuilding (temporary structure – 1960s). Now demolished.
61	Station HQ outbuilding (temporary structure – 1960s). Now demolished.
62	Guard house and postwar armoury.
	Also used as Fire HQ in 1960s.
64	Officers' Mess.
67	Cricket pavilion, constructed circa 1982.
82	Tennis Courts.
85	Playing field.
86	Playing field.
90	Parade square / car park.
91	Flagpole. Site of the Bloodhound missile 'Gate Guardian' to early 1970s.
92	Fire tender shed.

93	Wartime 'Night Flying Equipment Store'.
	7 AEF crew room, 1957-early 1990s.
95	Pyrotechnic store (ready use).
96	Radio Mast.
102	Wooden 'Spooner' hut used by 1936 Sqn ATC, mid 1960s to 1997.
106	Air raid shelter 'Stanton' type.
110	Air raid shelter 'Stanton' type.
114	Wooden hut used by NUAS to mid 1970s, then EM Wing ATC to 1997.
125	Use unknown. Timber hutting and demolished by mid 1970s.
126	Use unknown. Timber hutting and demolished by mid 1970s.
127	Wartime 'Grocery Store'.
	NAAFI shop, Barbers and Post office from 1965-1995.
	HQ 1936 Sqn ATC from 2001.

PAVCR	Portable Aerodrome Visual Control Room, 1997-2000.
NW	Signals Square.
CW	Car Wash, circa 1974-2000.
AC	Astra Cinema.
07	1960s Computer room extension to Guard House.
H	Hawker Hunter, gate guardian, 1975-1995.
V	Vickers Varsity, police training aid, 1976-1989.
T	Telephone boxes.
PA	Cedar Atlantica tree planted by Princess Anne, 1978.
S	Wartime air raid shelter, 'Stanton' type.
CG	Cricket ground.
SC	Squash courts.
SF	Sewage Farm, removed or covered over postwar, possibly early 1970s.
SH	Standby Set House / Power House.
	Demolished postwar and turned into Officers' Mess Car Park.
G	Officers' Garages.
GYM	Wartime gymnasium / Church.
	Used postwar as an indoor shooting range. Closed 1983. Demolished 2005.
TC	Tennis Courts.
PB4	Machine Gun Post or 'Pill Box No.4'.
CGS	Compressed Gas Storage area.
BP	Bulk Petrol Storage installation (Underground).
M	Possibly wartime ammunition magazine. Used by Police dogs 1975-1995.
FP	Wartime bomb fusing point.
FS	Underground food store outside Airmen's Mess.
CP	Checkpoint / Mini-Guardhouse.
DRDF	Digital Resolution Direction Finder.
Newton Gardens	Officers' Married Quarters
Trenchard Close	Airmen's Married Quarters
Friar Walk	Airmen's Married Quarters
Fairway Crescent	Airmen's Married Quarters
FARMLAND	Originally intended in wartime
	(1941) as the site for Hangar (Shed) No.6.

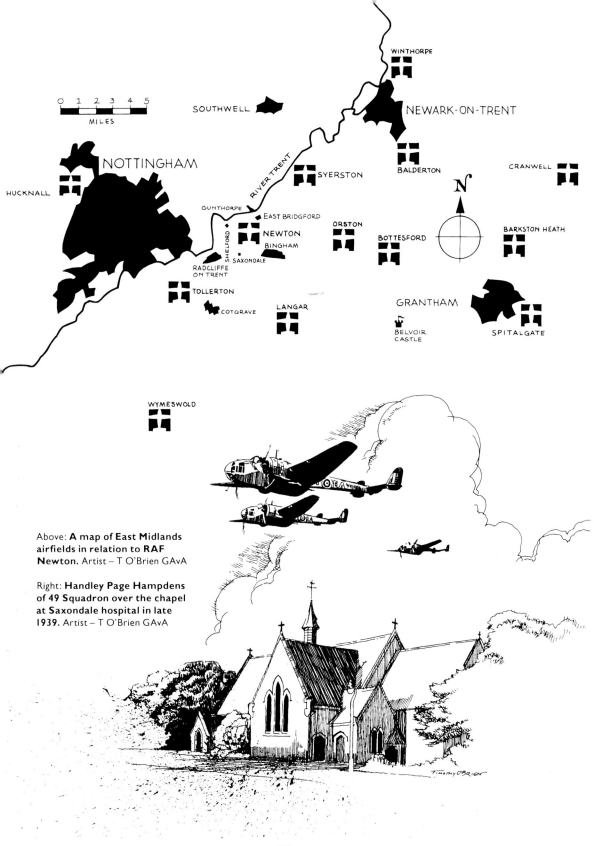

Above: **A map of East Midlands airfields in relation to RAF Newton.** Artist – T O'Brien GAvA

Right: **Handley Page Hampdens of 49 Squadron over the chapel at Saxondale hospital in late 1939.** Artist – T O'Brien GAvA

WINTHORPE

SOUTHWELL

NEWARK-ON-TRENT

NOTTINGHAM

HUCKNALL

RIVER TRENT

SYERSTON

BALDERTON

CRANWELL

N

GUNTHORPE

EAST BRIDGFORD

SHELFORD

NEWTON

ORSTON

BOTTESFORD

BARKSTON HEATH

BINGHAM

SAXONDALE

RADCLIFFE ON TRENT

TOLLERTON

COTGRAVE

LANGAR

GRANTHAM

BELVOIR CASTLE

SPITALGATE

WYMESWOLD

0 1 2 3 4 5
MILES

Happy Christmas!

An official white embossed Christmas card issued by RAF Newton; circa 1960; and one titled 'Last Post at Newton' published by the RAF Benevolent Fund in 2003.
M & D Sibley collection

BOROUGH OF RUSHCLIFFE

WELLINGTON AVENUE

Further Reading

Action Stations 2: Military airfields of Lincolnshire and the East Midlands
Bruce Barrymore Halpenny; Patrick Stephens Limited, 1981. ISBN 0-85059-484-7

Aeroplane Monthly, September 2006
'Under Starters Orders' article by Hugh F O'Neill

Airfield Review, Issue No.91, July 2001
'RAF Newton closes to flying' article by Aldon Ferguson; Airfield Research Group.

Alan Sillitoe's Nottinghamshire
Alan Sillitoe; Grafton books, 1987. ISBN 0 246 12852 6

Around the world at 90 Knots
Squadron Leader Bill Purchase MBE, 2000. ISBN 1 870530 01 2

Black Swan: A history of 103 Squadron RAF
Sid Finn, Newton; Edenbridge, Kent 1989. ISBN 1 872308 00 7

Bomber Squadrons of the RAF and their aircraft
Philip J R Moyes; Macdonald, London 1964. ISBN 356 01462 2

British Airfield Buildings, Volume Two: The Expansion and Inter-War Periods
Graham Buchan Innes; Midland Publishing, 2000. ISBN 1 85780 101 6

Fighter Squadrons of the RAF and their aircraft
John D Rawlings; Macdonald and Jane's. Revised edition 1976. ISBN 0 354 01028 X

Royal Air Force NEWS: RAF Newton by Gordon Skilling
Issue published on 22nd June 1990.

Royal Air Force NEWS: The Air Training Corps and 1936 Sqn ATC
Issue No.787 published 29th November 1991.

RAF Bomber Command Losses of the Second World War: Volume One, 1939-1940
W R Chorley; Midland Counties Publications. 1992. ISBN 0 904597 85 7

RAF Bomber Command Losses of the Second World War: Volume Two, 1941
W R Chorley; Midland Counties Publications. 1993. ISBN 0 904597 87 3

RAF Gate Guards
Jim Simpson and Kev Darling; Airlife Publishing 1992. ISBN: 1-85310-166-4.

Shelford and Newton: A thousand years of history
Pam Priestland; Shelford and Newton Parish Council 2000.

'White Eagles' – Memories from the Nottinghamshire Polish Air Force Community
Phil Barton; Nottinghamshire Living History Archive Millennium Award Scheme 2002.
ISBN 1-904102-25-5

Acknowledgements

I thought I knew Royal Air Force Newton reasonably well, that is until I started
this book back in 2001 and only then did I realise that I had only just 'scratched
the surface'! By studying official sources and interviewing those who served at
Newton, I feel that I have now been able to cover most aspects of the Station.
With this in mind, I am very grateful to all individuals and organisations who,
over the years have loaned material, solved mysteries, opened 'doors', contributed
information, anecdotes and personal stories, which have all made this book
possible. I apologise if I have inadvertently left anyone out, but most notably
I would like to mention the following:

Air Commodore Peter G Naz RAF (Retd);
Group Captain C B Adcock BA FIMGT RAF (Retd);
Group Captain Philip Langrill OBE RAF (Retd);
Group Captain John Laycock BA RAF (Retd);
Group Captain Roland Lloyd RAF (Retd);
Group Captain John Martin RAF (Retd);
Group Captain Hugh F O'Neill DFC & bar RAF (Retd);
Squadron Leader Norman Allen RAF (Retd);
Squadron Leader David Haller RAF (Retd);
Squadron Leader Bill Purchase MBE RAF (Rtd);
Squadron Leader John Rivers RAF (Retd);
Squadron Leader Mike Yarram, BSc, RAFR,
East Midlands Universities Air Squadron;
Wing Commander Edward Cartner RAF (Retd);
Wing Commander Phil Giles OBE, MCIPD, RAFVRT (Retd);
Wing Commander Ken Wallis MBE, Deng(hc), CEng, FRAeS, HFSETP, RAF (Retd);
Flt Lt John North RAFVRT (Retd);
Flt Lt Joe Clark RAFVRT (Retd);
Janet Greasley, Squadron Chairman, 1936 (Newton) Squadron Air Training Corps;
Tim Pearce, Assistant Librarian, Royal Air Force College Cranwell;
John Francis, General Manager, RAF Museum Cosford;

National Archives of Australia, Canberra;
Mike Smith, curator, Newark Air Museum;
Mick Blackman;
Rosalyn Blackmore;
Raymond and Louise Bratty;
Lloyd Brewer MBE;
Tim Chamberlin;
Kit Carpenter;
Karen Cheetham;
The Rt Hon Kenneth Clarke QC, MP;
Henry Clough;
Danielle Miles (nee Cameron);
Carl Bartz, CompAir Reavell;
Adam Davey;
Jim and Steve Elton;
David Fell, 103 Squadron Association;
James & Carole Fisher,
  Newton House Farm;
Alexsander Gertner;
Bob Goater;
Brian Goulding;
Margaret Goulder;
Lewin and Margaret Grant;
Richard Harcourt;
Bob Jones;
Mike King;
Jan Krupa;

Bart Luckhurst;
Jeffrey 'Errol' Manchester;
Brin Mason;
David Mumford;
Roger Miller, Beech Farm, Shelford;
Michael, Susan & Kerry O'Brien;
Desmond Penrose;
Milan Petrovic;
Kenneth Poxon;
Jeff Proudlock;
Chris Salter;
Margaret and David Sibley;
Reg Simpson;
Max Shortley;
Ted Shuvalski;
Nick Stroud, *Aeroplane Monthly*;
Jozef & Georgina Warchal;
Michael Turner PGAvA;
George Ward;
Charles Waterfall;
Len Watson;
Barrie Widdowson;
Ronald Wilbey;
Brian Whitaker;
Simon Whittle;
Stan Wright;
Norman J Yates.

...and Julie, George and Niamh for their patience!

The Author

"My association with Royal Air Force Newton began twenty-five years ago when I joined 1936 (Newton) Squadron of the Air Training Corps (ATC). Prior to that, my only connection was watching the Chipmunks and Bulldogs from the back garden of our house in Radcliffe-on-Trent and standing on the garden bench competing with my sister to get a better view of the Red Arrows during one of their pre-display season practice sessions.

Having left a tired Sea Scout unit to join the ATC at Newton I soon found plenty of challenges in a wealth of activities. Although practicing drill between the hangars, followed by Airmanship lessons on my second visit nearly put me off for good! Encouraged by my Dad to "Stick with it", I thankfully persevered and went on to enjoy my time with the ATC at Newton, reaching the rank of Cadet Warrant Officer before returning for a further stint as a Civilian Instructor before leaving in 1998. There are many precious memories of attending the Battle of Britain Air Days, flying and gliding. Plus humorous incidents such as looking back through the rear window of my Dad's Ford Cortina to see a dozen grinning Air Cadets peering in as they pushed us around the station helping to kick start the flat battery. And the time during the Miner's Strike when three off-duty civilian policemen jumped into my Dad's car after he had dropped me off at the main gate to attend the ATC, having mistaken him for a taxi and me for an airman! RAF Newton has played a vital part in my formative years to which I am grateful especially as my aviation art career was also launched here in the squadron's old wooden hut at the tender age of thirteen.

Over the years I have also been very fortunate to have flown as a passenger in various aircraft, many of which have an association with Newton such as the Tiger Moth biplane, DC-3 Dakota, Kirby Cadet MkIII glider, Chipmunk, Bulldog and most recently (August 2008) former Newton resident, Firefly G-BUUE which I flew in for an aerial photo-shoot of the station. This was the first time I had flown in Newton's former air-space since 1991 and I thought it was an apt moment to finish off the book as my tribute to RAF Newton and say farewell to an old friend."

Tim O'Brien GAvA,
Bingham, Nottingham. September, 2008.

Tim, a full member of the Guild of Aviation Artists was trained as a commercial artist upon leaving school by his father before going freelance in 1992. Today, Tim hand-produces a wide variety of illustration for industry, the collectables market and private individuals. He is married with two children and lives within sight of RAF Newton's hangars and water tower.

During the spring of 2009, Tim started work on his next book which will cover the history of Newton's close neighbour: Royal Air Force Syerston.

More details can be found on his website at: www.timobrienart.co.uk

ROYAL AIR FORCE NEWTON

Nottingham NG13 8HL

Tel. East Bridgford (0949) 20771 Ext 7212
GPTN ..... (Service use only)

Mr T O'Brien
... ...
... ...
Notts

Our Reference:
NEW/1014/1/P1

7 November 1994

Dear Mr O'Brien

ROYAL AIR FORCE NEWTON PLAQUES

Thank you for your recent letter requesting information on the sale of Royal Air Force Newton Plaques. The Station Plaque costs £11.50 and consists of a wooden shield bearing Newtons crest. Should you wish to purchase one please contact the undersigned to arrange a mutually convenient time to visit the Station.

Yours sincerely

A G..... .....
.....ying Of.....
.. Offi.....

The Shape of Things to Come?

During March 2009 work finally started on the long-awaited dualling of the A46 from Widmerpool to Farndon.

This impacted on Newton Gardens where four Officer's Married Quarters were demolished in mid-August to make way for the new road. The partially demolished property in this view taken in July 2009 was vandalised by arsonists circa 2005. The main contractor; Balfour Beatty also opened up this former 'Crash Gate' as an access road for their heavy plant equipment and personnel temporarily housed by No.5 Hangar, while the 'management' transformed the former SHQ into their 'Project Office'.

Meanwhile, on the Eco-Town 'front': local villagers celebrated on Thursday 16th July 2009 at the news that the former RAF site had been rejected as one of the first four Government backed 'Eco-Town' sites. But, landowners and developers at Newton vowed to forge ahead anyway with a scaled-down version instead. Campaigners now turned their attention to the proposed large scale gravel extraction around Shelford and Newton! The fight goes on...

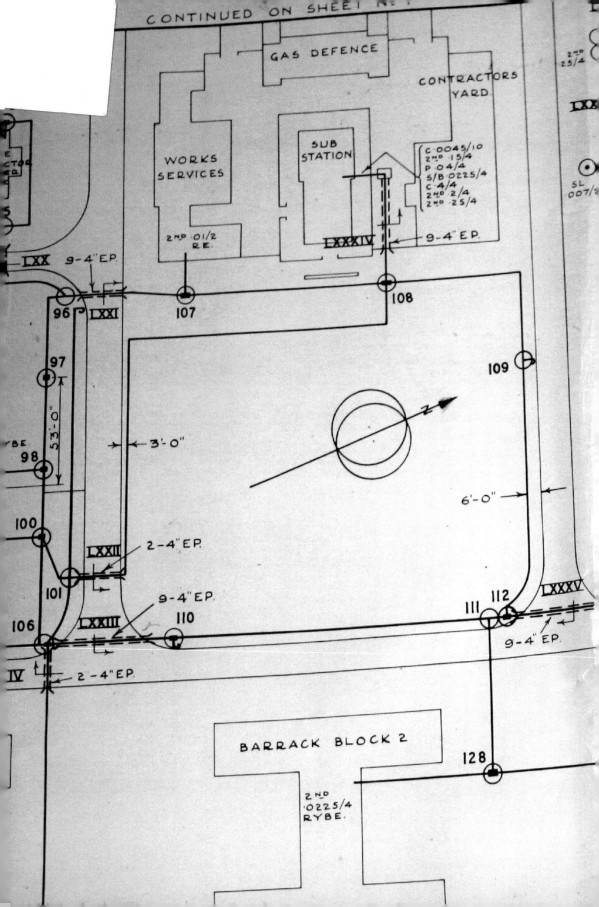

GAS DEFENCE

CONTRACTORS YARD

WORKS SERVICES

SUB STATION

C·0045/10
2ND 15/4
P 04/4
S/B 0225/4
C·4/4
2ND·2/4
2ND·25/4

9-4" E.P.

2ND 01/2
R.E.

LXXXIV

IXX

SL 007/

IXX 9-4"E.P.

96 IXXI

107

108

109

97

53'-0"

3'-0"

6'-0"

BE.

98

100

LXXII

2-4" E.P.

111 112 LXXXV

101

9-4"E.P.

110

106 LXXIII

9-4" E.P.

IV 2-4"E.P.

BARRACK BLOCK 2

128

2ND
·0225/4
RYBE.